How to get every Network Diagram question right on the PMP® Exam–
PMP Exam Prep Simplified Series of mini-books
50+ PMP® Exam Prep Sample Questions and Solutions on Network Diagrams

More books by
Aileen Ellis, PgMP, PMP

PMP Exam Simplified -5th Edition
Gain knowledge and confidence to pass the PMP Exam by utilizing over 1,000 sample
questions and detailed solutions (AME Group)

CAPM Exam Simplified -5th Edition
Gain knowledge and confidence to pass the CAPM Exam by utilizing over 800 sample
questions and detailed solutions (AME Group)

How to get every Contract Calculation Question right on the PMP® Exam –
PMP Exam Prep Simplified Series of mini-e-books
(50+ PMP® Exam Prep Sample Questions and Solutions
on Contract Calculations
(AME Group 2014)

How to get every Earned Value Question right on the PMP® Exam – PMP Exam Prep
Simplified Series of mini-e-books
(50+ PMP® Exam Prep Sample Questions and Solutions
on Earned Value Management.)
(AME Group 2014)

How to get every Financial Question right on the PMP® Exam -
PMP Exam Prep Simplified Series of mini-e-books
(50+ PMP® Exam Prep Sample Questions and Solutions
on NPV, IRR, ROI, Etc.)
(AME Group Coming late 2015)

How to get every Statistical based Question right on the PMP® Exam – PMP Exam Prep
Simplified Series of mini-e-books
(50+ PMP® Exam Prep Sample Questions and Solutions
on standard deviation, variance, probability, Etc.)
(AME Group Coming late 2015)

To Alex, Nick and Terry
For all your patience and support
With our books and our business

I _____, will acquire my PMP®
Certification by _____.

In preparation for this certification I will
review _____PMP® Sample
Questions per day for _____days.

In total I will complete a minimum of
1,000 sample questions before I attempt
the PMP® Exam.

With each and every sample question I will
not move past the question until I
understand why the right answer is right
and why each of the wrong answers are
wrong.

_____ *(signature)*

_____ *(date)*

Preface

In the last 16 years, I have helped over 10,000 project managers in my workshops obtain their PMP® credential. When they come into the workshop, the topic of Network Diagrams is typically a little scary.

After the exam, most of my students say that the exam was the hardest exam they have ever taken. When I ask them how they felt about the Network Diagram Questions on the exam they make comments such as:

"The diagrams on the exam were so easy compared to the Diagrams in your book."

Many will even say very quietly with a smile and a wink:

"I think I got every Network Diagram Question on the exam right".

I believe my students do so well on these questions because I just love teaching all topics to do with the PMP® Exam.

For me the best way to prepare for the exam is through hundreds, if not thousands of sample questions.

I hope these questions help you so much that you walk out of the PMP® Exam **with your PMP® Credential in hand** smiling and saying...

"I think I got every Network Diagram Question right."

About the Author

Aileen Ellis, PgMP®, PMP®, is The PMP® Expert. She is the owner and proudly the only instructor for AME Group Inc., a Registered Education Provider (REP®) through the Project Management Institute (PMI®). She personally instructs project managers to gain the confidence and knowledge to pass the PMP® Exam, the CAPM® Exam and the PgMP® Exam. She has helped more than 10,000 professionals obtain their PMP® and over 1,000 professionals obtain those coveted letters: CAPM®. Working with thousands of students from dozens of countries, Ms. Ellis has gained a thorough understanding of the ins and outs of the PMBOK® Guide, the exam content, and proven test-taking strategies.

Ms. Ellis began teaching Exam Preparation Courses in 1998. Over the years she has mastered how students learn best and has incorporated those lessons and methods into her books. Her approach is focused on understanding the Project Management Processes and their interactions, with limited memorization. Ms. Ellis not only leads workshops to help students study for and pass the CAPM®, PMP®, and PgMP® exams through review of content and hundreds of sample questions, she provides materials (books, sample questions) to other REP®s and PMI® Chapters to support their educational efforts.

How to Prepare for the PMP® Exam

Preparing for the PMP® can be overwhelming. Over the years I have helped over 10,000 participants in my face to face workshops pass the exam on their first try. I realize that not everyone has the opportunity, or the desire, to participate in one of my face to face workshops. Therefore I am developing products to help project managers around the world gain the knowledge and confidence to pass the exam without wasting time and money.

Print Books and E-books
While I really enjoy reading a print book I realize that some of you prefer e-books. Therefore as of July 2015 all of our current print books are now available in e-book format.

Here are some of the items available or in development. Please email me directly at aileen@amegroupinc.com so that I can make sure I am developing products that add value to you.

Mini Books- available at amazon.com
How to get Every Earned Value Question right on the PMP® Exam
How to get Every Contract Math Question right on the PMP® Exam
How to get Every Network Diagram Question right on the PMP® Exam
How to get Every Statistical Question right on the PM®P Exam (in development)
How to get Every Financial Question right on the PMP® Exam (in development)
How to get Every Math Question right on the PMP® Exam (in development)

Full Study Guides-available at amazon.com
PMP® Exam Simplified
CAPM® Exam Simplified

Online Courses- available at www.aileenellis.com
PMP® Exam with Aileen Online- 35 contact hours (in development)
CAPM® Exam with Aileen Online- 23 contact hours (in development)

Live Face to Face Programs- schedule at www.aileenellis.com
PMP® Exam Prep- Live with Aileen (public)
PMP® Exam Prep-Live with Aileen (at your worksite or PMI® Chapter)

Set Up of the book:

Part One- Some basic ideas on Network Diagrams and a short Video Class.

Part Two- 50+ Network Diagram Questions and Solutions. Do the questions one at a time. Learn from one question before you move on to the next question.

Terminology
In the book and on the PMP® Exam the following terms all have the same meaning:
- Float
- Total float
- Slack
- Total slack

In this book and on the PMP® Exam the following terms all have the same meaning when describing a path:
- Planned
- Anticipated
- Expected

In this book and on the PMP® Exam when listing the activities on a path we may use a plus sign or a minus sign to separate the activities. As an example the following two ways of listing a path have the same meaning:
- Activities A+B+D+F
- Activities A-B-D-F.

We list the path both ways as it could appear either way on the exam.

Difficulty:
Many of the questions in the book are representative of the difficulty of the questions on the PMP® Exam.

Some of the questions in this book are too hard to be representative of the PMP® Exam. I would rather readers feel my examples are harder than the real exam and for my readers to feel over prepared than under prepared for the exam.

Diagrams:
Some of the diagrams in the book and on the PMP® Exam are used multiple times. On the real exam, every time you see a network diagram you should ask if you have already seen the diagram in a different question. Follow the same logic in this book.

PART ONE

Some notes on Network Diagrams:
Network Diagrams:
One the PMP® Exam there are three different types of network diagrams:

- The precedence diagram (sometimes called activity on node)
- The activity on arrow diagram (sometimes called activity on line)
- The GERT diagram (GERT stands for Graphical Evaluation Review Technique)

Most, if not all of your questions will reference the precedence diagram.

The precedence diagraming method (PDM) produces precedence diagrams.

Precedence diagrams allow for four types of relationships:

- Finish to start relationships (the most common relationship)
- Finish to finish relationships
- Start to start relationships
- Start to finish relationships (the least common relationship)

The critical path method (CPM)- this is the method used to calculate the theoretical early start, early finish, late start, and late finish for each activity on the project schedule. These theoretical numbers tell us how much flexibility we have on the schedule and also the minimum project duration.

Several important definitions:
   The critical path:
   - the longest path through the network
   - the shortest amount of time to complete the project (the shortest project duration)
   - with CPM (critical path method) the critical path normally has zero total float during planning

Critical activity- any activity on the critical path.

Total float = float = total slack = slack- the amount of time an activity may be delayed without delaying the project finish date.
Total float= late finish – early finish.

Free float- the amount of time an activity may be delayed without delaying the earliest start of any successor.

Project float- the amount of time the project may be delayed without impacting an imposed end date.

Negative float- a project may have negative float. A negative float for the project means the amount of time required for the project is greater than the amount of time allocated.

Early start- theoretically the earliest an activity may start
Early finish- theoretically the earliest an activity may finish
Late start- theoretically the latest an activity may start
Late finish- theoretically the latest an activity may finish

EXAM TIP: The critical path method assumes unlimited resources.

Often when we do critical path calculations we use the notation shown below.

Early Start	Duration	Early Finish
	Activity Name	
Late Start	Float	Late Finish

If you see questions on the exam that ask about the duration of the critical path, the activities on the critical path, the float of an activity, the free float of an activity etc., you most likely will use the critical path method to solve.

In general to use the critical path method we:

1. Draw the network diagram (you may be given the diagram in the problem or given a table or word description). Label the activities including all the information provided to you, including duration.
2. Perform a forward pass to calculate the planned project duration and/or the planned critical path duration and/or free float.
3. Perform a backward pass to calculate float of activities and/or identify the critical path and/or the critical activities.

Describing this process in words can be difficult. I have attempted to do so on the next two pages.

Please go to: http://aileenellis.com/network-diagram-example-for-pmp-exam-and-capm-exam-from-aileen/

This free 10 minute online course will take you through the forward and backward pass step by step.
This online course is a critical part of this book and free to those who have purchased the book.

Forward Pass- Let's assume you have a network diagram. To perform a forward pass we begin at the left. I usually work in columns.

Step 1. The early start of the first activity is 1. Write 1 on the diagram in the top left corner of Activity A.

Step 2. The early finish is equal to the early start plus the duration minus 1. In this example for Activity A the Early finish = 1 + 5 – 1 = 5. The early finish goes in the top right corner of the activity.

Step 3. The early start of the next activity (the successor activity) is 1 plus the early finish of the current activity. For Activity B the early start is 5 + 1 = 6. The same is true for Activity C.

(You need to go back to Step 2 to determine the early finish of Activity B and Activity C.)

Step 4. Going forward if more than one path converges into a single activity the early start of that activity is 1 plus the largest early finish found on any of the converging paths. When determining the early start of Activity E will look at the two predecessors. Activity B has a larger early finish than Activity C. Therefore to determine the early start of Activity E will look at the early finish of Activity B only. Early start of Activity E = Early finish of Activity B (14 days) plus 1 day = 15.

Step 5. Continue until you have completed the entire forward pass.

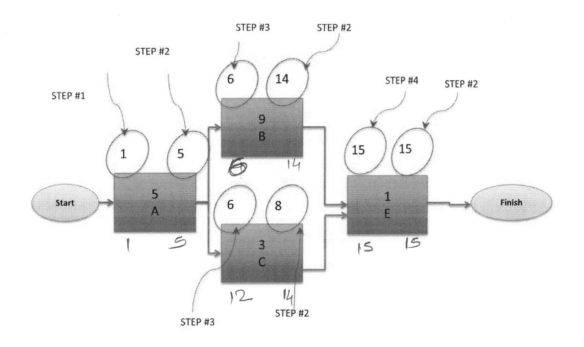

Backward Pass- Lets continue based on the forward pass just completed. To perform a backward pass begin at the right and move to the left in columns.

Step 1. The late finish of the last activity (Activity E) is the same as the early finish of the last activity. Just copy the early finish of the last activity and write it in the late finish position- the bottom right of the activity.

Step 2. The late start of an activity is equal to the late finish minus the duration plus 1. For Activity E the late start = 15 -1 +1 = 15.

Step 3. The late finish of any immediately preceding activity is the late start of the current activity minus 1. For Activity B the late finish = 15 (which is the late start of Activity E) – 1 = 14.

Step 4. Going backwards if an activity has two successors we determine its late finish by taking the smallest late start of the successors and subtracting one. For Activity A there are 2 successors (Activity B and C). Activity B has the smallest late start. The late finish of Activity A = 6 (the late start of Activity B) – 1 = 5.

Step 5. Continue until you have completed the entire backward pass.

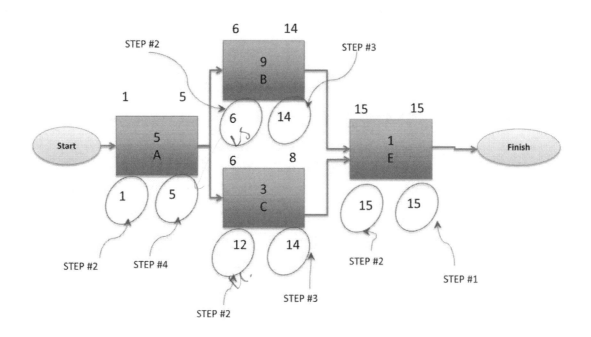

Forward passes with complex relationships:

Finish to start (FS) relationships- this is the most common relationship. All relationships are assumed to be finish to start unless otherwise stated. Activity A must finish before Activity B may start.
Example: we finish writing code before we start testing code.

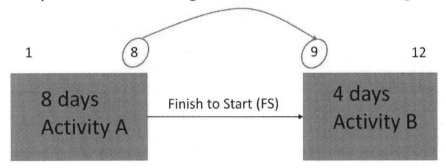

Finish to finish (FF) relationships- Activity A must finish before Activity B may finish. Example: I must finish cooking the meal before I may finish serving the meal on the table.
You may not like where we drew the line between A and B for a finish to finish relationship. On the exam we expect the line to be drawn and labeled like this figure.

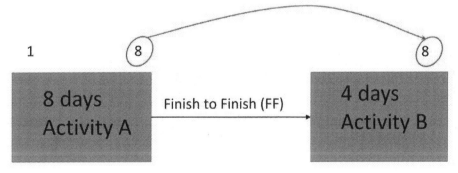

Start to start (SS) relationships- activity A must start before activity B may start. I must start washing my dishes before I may start drying my dishes.

You may not like where we drew the line between A and B for a start to start relationship. On the exam we expect the line to be drawn and labeled like this figure.

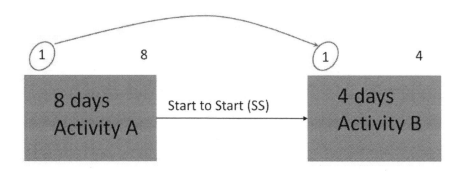

Start to finish (SF) relationships- Activity G must start before Activity H may finish. This is the least common of all relationships and many of us will not use the relationship in any of our network diagrams. Example: the night security guard must start his shift before the day security guard may finish his shift. We don't need to worry about the forward and backward pass for this relationship on the exam so we will skip over it here as well.

Leads and Lags:

See how the total duration gets affected by leads & lags

Let's view a logical relationship with no leads and lags.

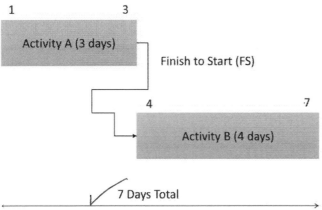

Leads: A lead is a modification in a logical relationship that allows the acceleration of a successor activity. In the following diagram Activity D is allowed to accelerate 2 days. In other words Activity D may start 2 days before Activity C finishes.

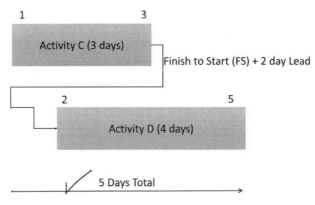

Lags: A lag is a modification in a logical relationship that forces the delay of a successor activity. In the following diagram Activity F cannot start until 2 days after Activity E has finished.

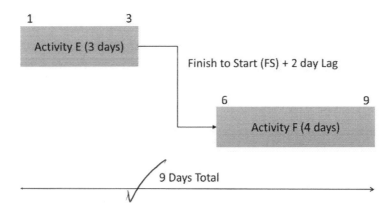

The arrow diagraming method (ADM) produces activity on arrow (AoA) diagrams. Activity on arrow (AOA) diagrams allow for only finish to start relationships.

In these diagrams the arrow represents:
- the activity and
- the precedence

These diagrams may also use dummy activities. Dummy activities ensure that all logical dependencies are represented accurately. Dummy activities have zero duration.

The circles (often called nodes) represent events that require no time or resources.

The nodes may have letters or numbers in the node. If there are numbers in the node like our example below the numbers do *not* represent durations. The numbers are names for the node. Example: Node 1.

Primary rule: All activities that enter a node must be completed before any activity leaving the node may be started.

In the diagram below Activity A must finish before Activity B may start.

Activity A and Activity D must finish before Activity C may start. The dummy activity tells us that Activity A must finish before Activity C may start.

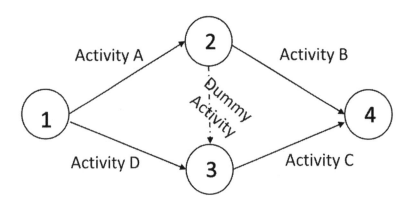

Graphical evaluation review technique (GERT) is used to produce GERT diagrams. GERT is a network analysis technique that allows for probabilistic treatment of the network logic and estimation of activity durations.

GERT is not common because of the complexity of GERT.
GERT allows for conditional statements and loops between activities.
Monte Carlo simulation is often used to model GERT.

On the PMP® Exam GERT is more likely to be a wrong answer than a right answer. Let's look at the diagram below. The diagram looks like a flow chart. Imagine this flow chart with the feedback loop being part of your schedule. Can you see how the use of GERT may be very complicated in a schedule?

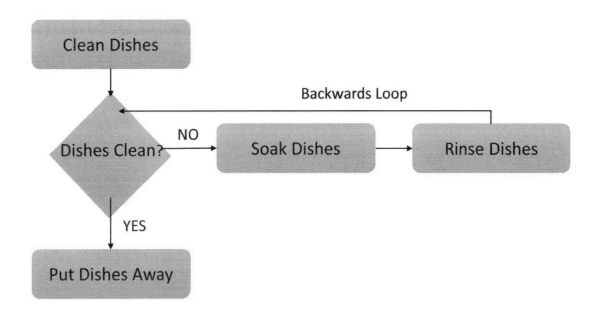

Statistical Ideas related to Network Diagrams:

(margin note: Formulas:)

(circled 1) Three Point Estimating
- Simple Average (Triangular Distribution)
- PERT (Beta Distribution)

(circled 2) Activity
- Standard Deviation $= (P - O) \div 6$
- Variance $= (SD)^2$

Path
- Standard Deviation
- Variance.

(handwritten right margin:)
Duration uncertainty $= P - O$
※ Pessimistic estimate will always be more than optimistic

We will take these ideas one at a time. Realize much more information can be found on these topics in my book: *How to get every Statistical Question right on the PMP Exam.*

(circled 1) **Three Point Estimating for an activity**

When estimating activity durations or costs the accuracy of a single estimate may not be good enough. At that point we may go to a three point estimate. The three point estimate looks at the:
- Most likely Estimate (ML)
- Pessimistic Estimate (P)- sometimes called worst case
- Optimistic Estimate (O)-sometimes call best case

To calculate duration (or cost) estimates with three points we may use:
- the simple average (sometimes called the Triangular distribution)

Or
- The PERT estimate (sometimes called the Beta distribution).

Simple Average estimate = (P+ML+O) ÷ 3.
PERT estimate = (P + 4ML + O) ÷ 6.

Calculate the simple average and the PERT for Activity A, B, C.

Activity	P	ML	O	Simple Avg. (Triangular Distribution)	PERT Est. (Beta Distribution)
A	32	22	18		
B	26	12	10		
C	28	14	12		

Activity	P	ML	O	Simple Avg. (Triangular Distribution)	PERT Est. (Beta Distribution)
A	32	22	18	24	23
B	26	12	10	16	14
C	28	14	12	18	16

Standard Deviation and Variance for an activity.

Standard Deviation is a measure of the amount of variation we have in a set of data. The larger the standard deviation the larger the variation. The smaller the standard deviation the small the variation.
Variance is Standard Deviation squared.

We will begin looking at one activity.

Standard Deviation = | (pessimistic - optimistic) ÷ 6|.
Standard Deviation = | (P-O) ÷ 6|.
Variance = (SD)^2

Variance = standard deviation squared

For activity D, E and F calculate the SD and Variance.

Activity	P	ML	O	SD	Variance
Activity D	48	22	12		
Activity E	30	14	6		
Activity F	39	21	9		

Activity	P	ML	O	SD	Variance
Activity D	48	22	12	6	36
Activity E	30	14	6	4	16
Activity F	39	21	9	5	25

On the Exam you are likely to be asked to calculate the Standard Deviation for an activity or the variance for an activity. It is no harder than what you just did for Activity D, E and F.

The tricky part and where someone would use this in real life is when we apply these ideas not just to an activity but to an entire path.

The next example is possible for the exam but not very likely. Therefore if you get it GREAT.
If you don't understand these ideas the first time, don't worry. If after a few times you still don't understand these ideas just move on. Come back to this content only after you really understand all the other ideas in this book.

(2) Standard Deviation and Variance for a path.

Sample Question: MOST LIKELY THIS QUESTION IS TOO HARD TO BE REPRESENTATIVE OF THE EXAM.

You are managing a project to rebuild a bridge over the River Nile in Egypt. There are four activities left on the critical path. Activity A has a duration uncertainty of 30 days. Activity B has a duration uncertainty of 24 days.   Activity C has a duration uncertainty of 12 days. Activity D has a duration uncertainty of 12 days.   Assume calculations are based on +/- 3 standard deviations. What is the duration uncertainty of the overall remaining path?

Solution: each element of this solution explains one area in our table.
To solve we usually use the following steps:
1. Determine duration uncertainty for each activity from pessimistic and optimistic numbers. We don't need to do this as it was a given.
    - Duration Uncertainty = P-O
2. Determine the Standard Deviation for each activity.
    - One SD = | (P-O)/6|.
3. Determine the variance of each activity
    - Variance = $(SD)^2$
4. Calculate the Project Variance for the remaining path
5. Determine the Standard Deviation for the remaining path
6. Determine duration uncertainty for the remaining path

Activities	P	O	Step 1 Duration Uncertainty	Step 2 One SD	Step3 Variance
Activity A			30	5	25
Activity B			24	4	16
Activity C			12	2	4
Activity D			12	2	4

Step 4	Variance for Path	Add individual variances together	=25+16+4+4= 49
Step 5	Standard Deviation for path	Square root of the path variance	Square root of 49 = 7
Step 6	Duration Uncertainty for path=	Same as +/-3 SD. Therefore multiple one standard deviation by 6.	7 * 6 = 42 days

Crashing

Crashing is adding additional resources to the critical path in order to shorten the length of the project.

A few rules about crashing:

1. Only crash activities on the critical path ＊_crash only critical_
2. Crash the activities on the critical path that save the most amount of time for the least amount of cost
3. Crash an early activity instead of a later activity if they have the same amount of time saved for the same cost

PART TWO

Question #1.

From the figure below what is the planned <u>project duration</u>? Assume the durations are in days.

a. 21 days
b. 24 days
c. 25 days ✓
d. 35 days

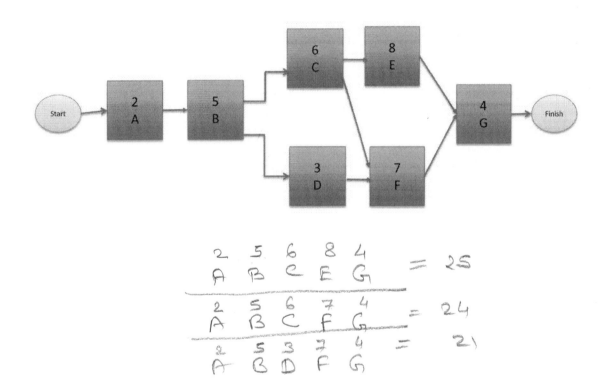

2 5 6 8 4
A B C E G   = 25

2 5 6 7 4
A B C F G   = 24

2 5 3 7 4
A B D F G   = 21

Solution #1.

Answer (c) is the best answer.

There are two methods to determine the anticipated project duration.

Method One:
List all the paths and then determine the longest path (the critical path).

A-B-C-E-G = 2+5+6+8+4 = 25
A-B-C-F-G = 2+5+6+7+4 = 24
A-B-D-F-G = 2+5+3+7+4 = 21.

The longest path (in days) is 25 days. Therefore the projected project duration is 25 days.

Method Two:
Some people would say the harder way to solve the problem is to use the critical path method. Here is the solution using critical path. Again we see the same answer of 25 days.

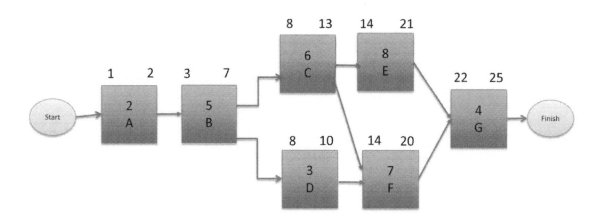

Question #2.

From the figure below what is the planned duration of the critical path? Assume the durations are in days.

a. 43 days
b. 24 days
c. 22 days
d. 18 days

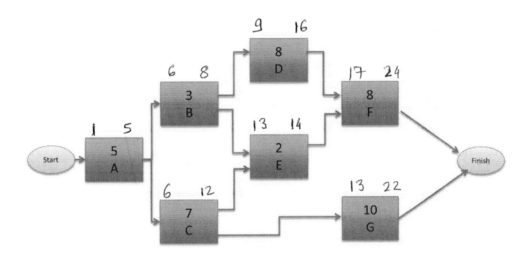

Solution # 2.

Answer (b) is the best answer.

There are two methods to determine the anticipated project duration and or the critical path.

Method One:
List all the paths and then determine the longest path (the critical path).

A-B-D-F = 5+3+8+8 =24
A-B-E-F = 5+3+2+8 = 18
A-C-E-F = 5+7+2+8 = 22
A-C-G = 5+7+10 =22

Therefore the critical path is A-B-D-F = 24 days.

Method Two:
The other method to solve is to perform a forward pass using the critical path method.

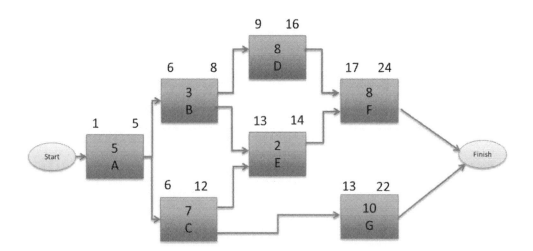

Question # 3.

From the figure below what is the anticipated length of the project?

a. 27 days
b. 28 days
c. 32 days
d. 54 days

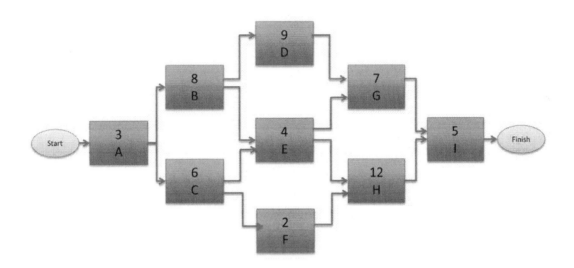

Solution # 3.

Answer (c) is the best answer.

There are two methods to determine the anticipated project duration and or the critical path.

Method One:
List all the paths and then determine the longest path (the critical path). This diagram is complicated. Most likely I would not use the "easy method" here because I do not want to miss any paths.
Paths:
A+B+D+G+I = 3+8+9+7+5 = 32 (Longest path is anticipated length of project.)
A+B+E+G+I = 3+8+4+7+5 = 27
A+C+E+G+I = 3+6+4+7+5 = 25
A+C+E+H+I = 3+6+4+12+5 = 30
A+C+F+H+I = 3+6+2+12+5 = 28

Method Two:
Therefore I would use the critical path method- forward pass to solve this problem.

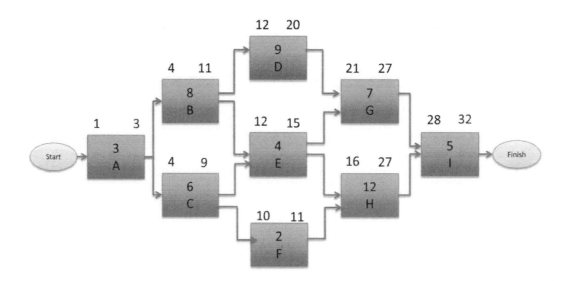

Question #4.

You have a project with the following activities:
Activity A begins after the start of the project and has a duration of 5 days. Activity B with a duration of 4 days and Activity D with a duration of 7 days both have Activity A as a predecessor. Activity C with a duration of 3 days is a successor to Activity B. Activity E with a duration of 6 days is a successor to both Activity B and D. Activity H with a duration of 2 days is a successor to both Activity C and Activity E. Activity E also has Activity F with a duration of 8 days as a successor. Activity I with a duration of 9 days is a successor to both Activity H and Activity F. The project finishes after Activity I is completed.

.

The planned duration of the project is:

a. 20 days
b. 26 days
c. 35 days
d. 37 days

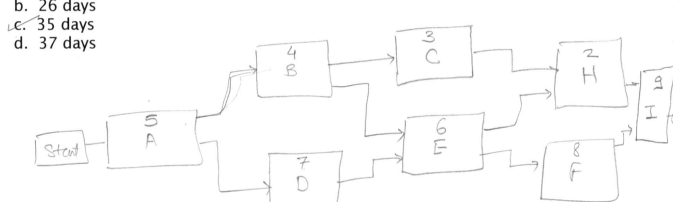

① $\overset{5}{A}\ \overset{4}{B}\ \overset{3}{C}\ \overset{2}{H}\ \overset{9}{I} = 23$

② $\overset{5}{A}\ \overset{4}{B}\ \overset{6}{E}\ \overset{2}{H}\ \overset{9}{I} = 26$

③ $\overset{5}{A}\ \overset{4}{B}\ \overset{6}{E}\ \overset{8}{F}\ \overset{9}{I} = 32$

④ $\overset{5}{A}\ \overset{7}{D}\ \overset{6}{E}\ \overset{2}{H}\ \overset{9}{I} = 29$

⑤ $\overset{5}{A}\ \overset{7}{D}\ \overset{6}{E}\ \overset{8}{F}\ \overset{9}{I} = 35$

Solution # 4.

Answer (c) is the best answer.

There are two methods to determine the anticipated project duration and or the critical path.

Method One:
List all the paths and then determine the longest path (the critical path).
A-B-C-H-I = 5+4+3+2+9 = 23
A-B-E-H-I = 5+4+6+2+9 = 26
A-B-E-F-I = 5+4+6+8+9 = 32
A-D-E-H-I = 5+7+6+2+9 = 29
A-D-E-F-I = 5+7+6+8+9 = 35

The longest path is 35 days. Therefore 35 days is the anticipated duration of the project (and of the critical path).

Method Two:
To solve using the critical path method we perform a forward path.

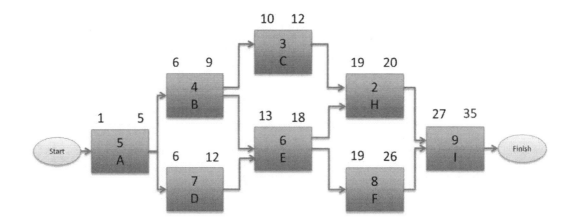

Question #5.

Based on the following diagram, what is the anticipated duration of the project?

a. 27 days
b. 20 days
c. 21 days
d. 26 days

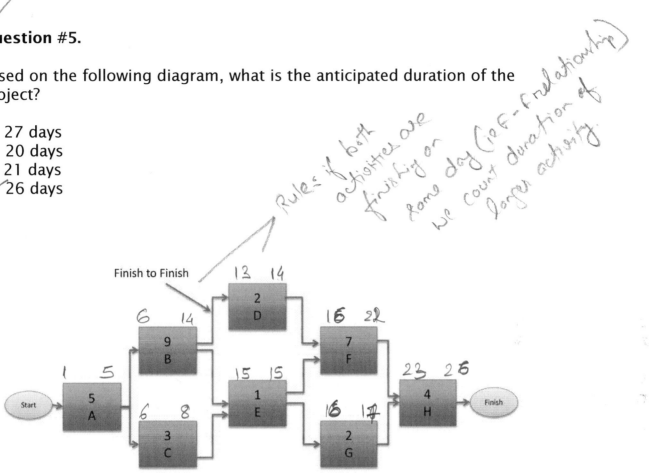

Rules if both activities are finishing or some day (ie f-f relationship) we count duration of larger activity

Finish to Finish

Solution # 5.

Answer (d) is the best answer.

There are two methods to determine the anticipated project duration and or the critical path.
Method One:
List all the paths and then determine the longest path (the critical path).

A-B-D-F-H= 5 +9+0+7+4 = 25. Note: (we do not add D's duration since B to D is a finish to finish). We take the large of the two numbers.

A-B-E-F-H = 5+9+1+7+4 = 26
A-B-E-G-H = 5+9+1+2+4 = 21
A-C-E-F-H = 5+3+1+7+4 = 20
A-C-E-G-H = 5+3+1+2+4 = 15

Therefore the anticipated length of the project will be the longest path (the critical path) with a duration of 26 days.

Method Two:
The other way to solve the problem is to use the critical path method.

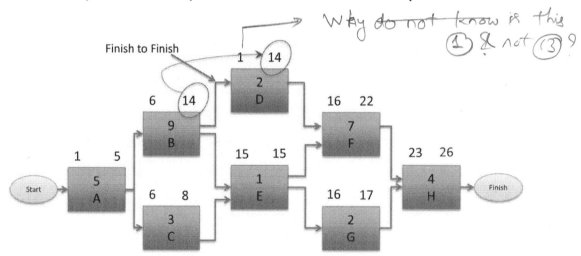

[handwritten note] Why do not know is this ① & not ③ ?

Question # 6.

Based on the table below what is the anticipated free float of Activity D?

a. 3 days
b. 4 days
c. 6 days
d. 14 days

Activity	Predecessor	Duration in Days
Activity A	Start	5 days
Activity B	Activity A	3 days
Activity C	Activity A plus 3 day lag	7 days
Activity D	Activity B	6 days
Activity E	Activity B and Activity C	2 days
Activity F	Activity D and Activity E	8 days
Finish	Activity F	Not applicable

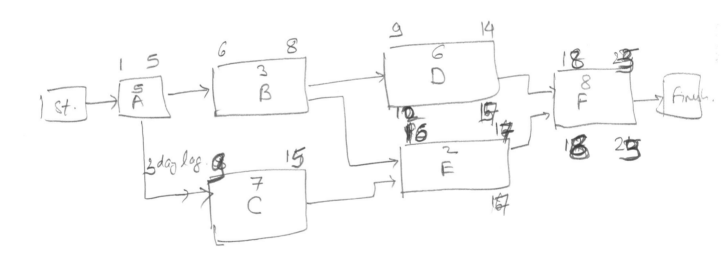

24-8+1=

Solution #6.

Answer (a) is the best answer.

To calculate free float it is easiest to begin by drawing the network diagram. Once we have the diagram we perform a forward pass.
Free Float of Activity D = Early Start of Activity F minus Early Finish of Activity D minus 1.
Free Float of Activity D = 18-14-1 = 3 days.

. Tricky areas:
- Let's look at the early start of Activity C. Activity A has an early finish of day 5. If the relationship of Activity A to C was just finish to start Activity C would have an early start of 6 days. Since we have a 3 day lag we add 3 days to the early start of 6 days to get an early start of 9 days. Remember that lags delay the successor.

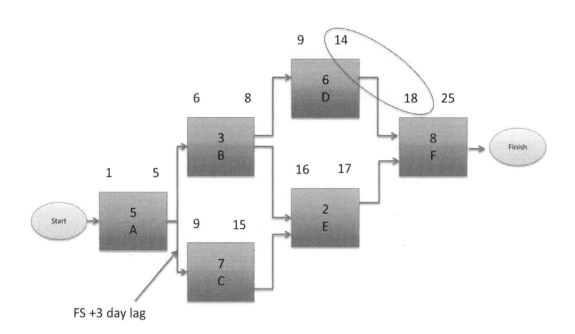

Question #7.

The project schedule shows a planned duration of 47 weeks. After careful review management has decided that the project must finish within 42 weeks. They ask you and your team to develop a plan to crash the schedule based on cost. There are five activities on the critical path that can be crashed. Activity A has a duration of 8 weeks and can be shortened by 2 weeks for a cost of $4,000. Activity F has a duration of 9 weeks and can be shortened by 4 weeks for a cost of $16,000. Activity J has a duration of 12 weeks and can be shortened by 1 week for a cost of $2,000. Activity K has a duration of 5 weeks and can be shortened by 2 weeks for a cost of $2,000. Activity R has a duration of 8 weeks and can be shortened by 3 weeks for a cost of $9,000.

The activities that should be crashed are:

a. Activity A and Activity R 13k
b. Activity K and Activity R 11k
c. Activity A and Activity J and Activity K 8k
d. Activity F and Activity J 18.

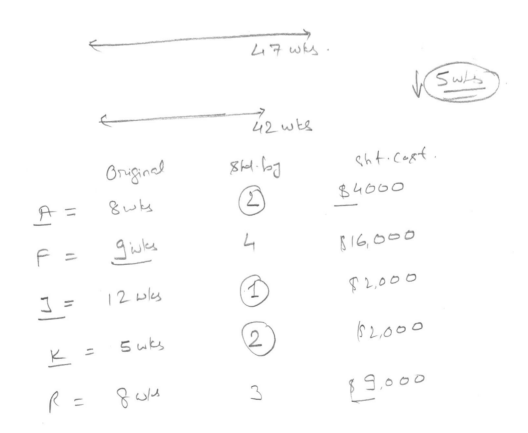

Solution #7.

Answer (c) is the best answer.

There is a lot of data in this question. When crashing we want to save the most amount of time for the least amount of money. For the Exam I most likely would create a table like the one below to help me easily solve this problem.

	Current Duration	Weeks saved by crashing	Cost of crashing	Cost/week of crashing
Activity A	8 weeks	2 weeks	$ 4,000	$ 2,000
Activity F	9 weeks	4 weeks	$ 16,000	$ 4,000
Activity J	12 weeks	1 week	$ 2,000	$ 2,000
Activity K	5 weeks	2 weeks	$ 2,000	$ 1,000
Activity R	8 weeks	3 weeks	$ 9,000	$ 3,000

Once I have the table I know I need to save five weeks for the least amount of money.

Answer (a) will save me 5 weeks for $13,000.
Answer (b) will save me 5 weeks for $11,000.
Answer (c) will save me 5 weeks for $8,000.
Answer (d) will save me 5 weeks for $18,000.

Answer (c) is the best answer.

 A few rules about crashing:

1. Only crash activities on the critical path
2. Crash the activities on the critical path that save the most amount of time for the least amount of cost
3. Crash an early activity instead of a later activity if they have the same amount of time saved for the same cost

Question #8.

As you are developing your project schedule it is suggested that you use PERT to estimate activity durations. You go to the engineer performing Activity A and ask her for her estimates. She states that best-case Activity A can be completed in 20 days. Most likely Activity A will take 25 days and worst-case Activity A will take 48 days. What is the PERT estimate you should use when building your schedule?

a. 20 days
b. 25 days
c. 28 days
d. 48 days

A   20   ML 25   P 48

$$\frac{20 + 100 + 48}{6}$$

$$\frac{20 + 4(25) + 48}{6}$$

Solution #8.

Answer (c) is the best answer.

PERT = (P+4ML+O) ÷ 6
P = pessimistic (worst case in the example)
ML = most likely
O = optimistic (best case in this example)

PERT = (48 + (4*25) +20) ÷ 6
PERT = 28 days

Question #9.

The complexity of your projects and your schedules has continued to grow over the last few years. At this point you now need to be able to look at your network logic from a probabilistic standpoint. You need network diagrams that allow for feedback looks. Therefore you most likely will need to utilize:

a. graphical evaluation and review technique (GERT).
b. critical path method (CPM)
c. program evaluation and review technique (PERT)
d. Critical chain method

Solution #9.

Answer (a) is the best answer.

GERT stands for graphical evaluation review technique. GERT is rarely used today. It allows for feedback loops and a probabilistic view of our network diagrams. GERT adds much complexity to our project schedules and therefore should only be used when the added value is worth the added complexity.

The critical path method is a scheduling method that helps us estimate the length of the project. The critical path method also helps us estimate the amount and location of schedule flexibility. This information allows us to focus on the critical path and make good decisions related to project trade-offs.

PERT stands for program evaluation review technique. PERT allows us to incorporate three estimates (pessimistic, most likely and optimistic) when estimating the expected time of an activity. We would not associate feedback looks with PERT.

The critical chain method is a scheduling technique that utilizes buffers on feeding paths and the critical path to account for limited resources and uncertainty.

When you have uncertainty & limited resources use chain method to add buffers.

Question #10.

From the table below what is the anticipated project duration?

a. 25 days
b. 29 days
c. 32 days
d. 42 days

Activity	predecessor	Duration
B	Start	8 days
D	Activity B	6 days
E	Activity B plus 7 day lag	2 days
F	Activity D and Activity E	8 days
G	Activity E plus 3 day lead	9 days
H	Activity F and Activity G	4 days

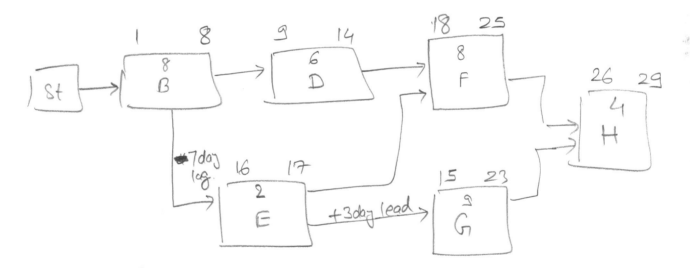

Solution #10.

Answer (b) is the best answer.

There are two methods to determine the anticipated project duration.
Method One: List all the paths and then determine the longest path.
B+D+F+H = 8+6+8+4 = 26 days
B+7day lag +E + F + H = 8+7+2+8+4 = 29 days
B+7day lag + E + (-3 days) +G + H = 8+7+2-3+9+4 = 27 days
The path of 29 days is the longest path and the anticipated project duration.
Method Two: Use the critical path method. Perform a forward pass.
Let's look at the early start of Activity E. Activity B has an early finish of day 8. If the relationship of Activity B to E was just finish to start Activity E would have an early start of 9 days. Since we have a 7 day lag we add 7 days to the early start of 9 days to get an early start of 16 days. Remember that lags delay the successor.
Let us look at the early start of Activity G. Activity E has an early finish of day 17. If Activity E to Activity G was a normal finish to start Activity G would have an early start of day 18. Since we have a 3 day lead we subtract 3 from day 18 and now have an early start of Activity G of day 15. Remember that leads accelerate he successor.

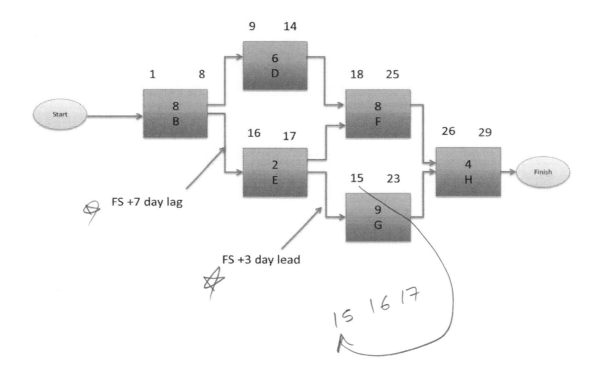

15 16 17

Question #11.

From the figure below what is the total float of Activity C? Assume durations in days.

a. 0 days
b. 1 day
c. 3 days
d. 6 days

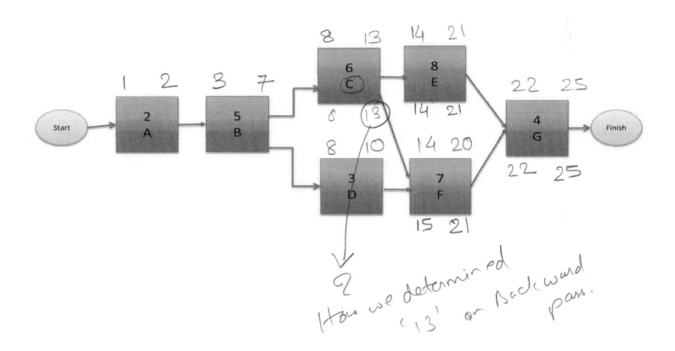

Solution #11.

Answer (a) is the best answer.

Remember the phrases total float, total slack, float and slack mean the same thing in this context.
To determine the float of an activity in general I prefer to perform a backward pass. We must perform a forward pass before we may perform a backward pass.

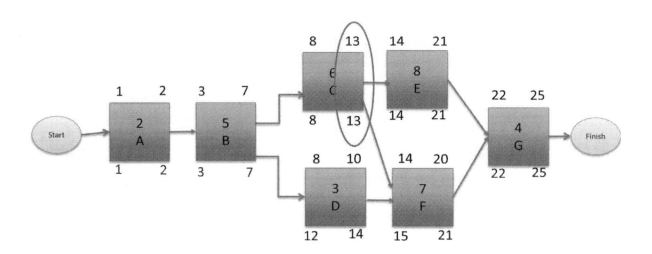

Question #12.

As the project manager you are working with team members to estimate activity durations. The engineer who will be responsible for Activity A states that most likely it will take 31 days to complete Activity A. Best case it may be completed in 25 days and worst case it could take as long as 43 days. The standard deviation for Activity A is:

a. 3 days
b. 9 days
c. 18 days
d. 31 days

$$O \qquad M \cdot L \qquad P$$

$$25 \qquad 31 \qquad 43$$

$$SD = \frac{P - O}{6} \quad = \quad \frac{43 - 25}{6} = \frac{18}{6} = 3.$$

$$SD = SD^2$$

$$SD = \frac{P - O}{6.}$$

Solution #12.

Answer (a) is the best answer.

Standard Deviation (SD)

SD = |(P-O) ÷ 6|
P = pessimistic (worst case in this example)
O = optimistic (best case in this example)

SD = | (43 – 25) ÷ 6 |
SD = | (18) ÷ 6 |
The Standard Deviation =3 days.

Question # 13.

From the diagram below what is the free float of Activity C?

a. 4 days
b. 2 days
c. 1 day
d. 0 days

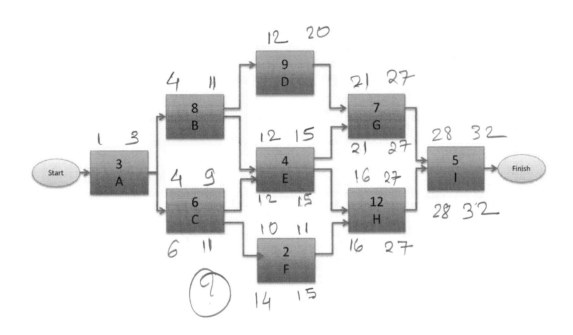

Solution #13.

Answer (d) is the best answer.

To calculate free float of an activity we use the critical path method. We only need to perform a forward pass to determine free float.

Free Float of Activity C = Early Start of Activity F minus Early Finish of Activity C minus 1
FF of C = 10 – 9 - 1
FF of C = 0.
Notice we did not look at Activity E. Remember my definition of Free Float. Free Float is how much an activity may slip before affecting the earliest start of any successor. Activity F has an earlier early start than Activity E.

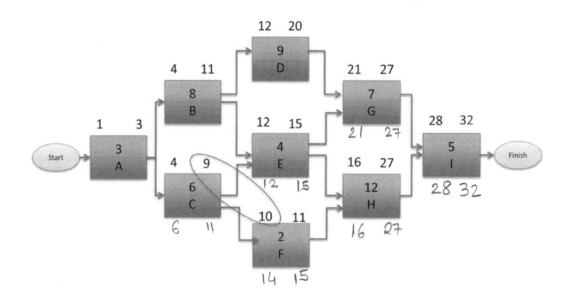

Question #14.

You are working with your project management staff to determine dependencies between activities. You have determined the following:
Activity A can start at the beginning of the project and has an estimated duration of 5 days.
Activity B can start after Activity A finishes and has an estimated duration of 3 days.
Activity C can start after Activity A finishes and has an estimated duration of 7 days.
Activity E can start only after both Activity B and Activity C are finished and has an estimated duration of 6 days.
Activity F can start after Activity E finishes and has an estimated duration of 9 days.
Activity G can start after Activity E starts and has an estimated duration of 12 days.
Activity H can start only after both Activity F and Activity G have finished and has a duration of 4 days. Activity H is the last activity of the project.

What is the anticipated project duration?

a. 27 days
b, 31 days
c, 33 days
d. 35 days

Solution #14.

Answer (b) is the best answer.

There are two methods to determine the anticipated project duration and or the critical path. Usually the easier way is to list the paths and then determine the length of the longest path. This question is a little different.

Method One: List all the paths and then determine the longest path.
Paths:
A-B-E-F-H = 5+3+6+9+4 = 27
A-B-E-G (Start to Start)-H = 5+3+12+4 = 24
A-C-E-F-H =5+7+6+9+4 = 31
A-C-E-G (Start to Start)-H =5+7+12+4 = 28

Notice when we have a start to start relationship we only count the duration of the longest activity. As an example Activity E and Activity G have a start to start relationship. The planned duration of Activity E is 6 days. The planned duration of Activity G is 12 days. Therefore when determining the anticipated length of the path we take the larger number of 12 days. Does this make sense with a start to start relationship?

Method Two. Critical Path Method.

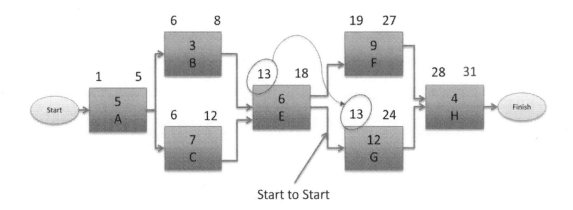

Start to Start

Question #15.

Based on the following diagram, what is the free float of Activity D?

a. 0 days
b. 1 day
c. 2 days
d. 4 days

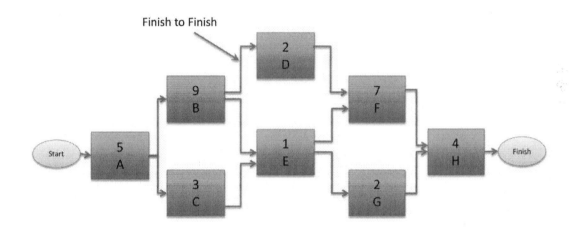

Solution #15.

Answer (b) is the best answer.

To solve for free float we need to perform a forward pass on the network diagram. We do not need to perform a backward pass on the network to solve for free float.

Free Float of Activity D = Early Start of Activity F minus Early Finish of Activity D minus 1
Free Float of Activity D = 16 – 14 - 1
Free Float of Activity D = 1 day.

Were you able to determine the early finish of Activity D? Since the relationship between Activity B and Activity D is finish to finish we take the early finish of Activity B (which is day 14) and make that also the early finish of Activity D.

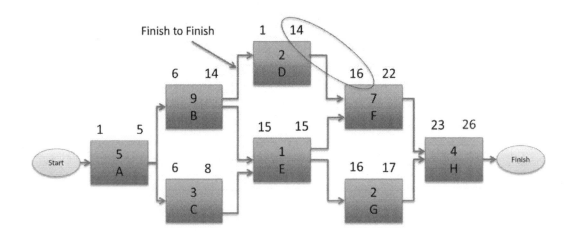

Question #16.

In the diagram below all durations are in weeks. As an example Activity A has a planned duration of 5 weeks. What is the total float of Activity F?

a. 18 weeks
b. 16 weeks
c. 14 weeks
d. 0 weeks

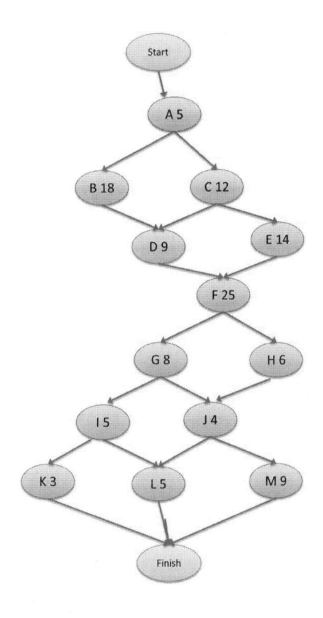

Solution # 16.

Answer (d) is the best answer.

Wow. What a diagram. Realize that network diagrams may be drawn many different ways. The convention is to use boxes for precedence diagrams. There is no reason though that someone could not draw the diagram with circles or ovals or any shape.
Did you go ahead and complete a forward pass to solve this problem? If you did that was a lot of work, a lot of wasted work. Let's look at Activity F. Can you determine just from looking at the diagram that Activity F must be on the critical path? During planning the total float of any activity on the critical path is zero unless than is an imposed end date.

No need to perform a forward pass on this diagram.

Question #17.

Based on your experience you realize there are many types of estimates that may be used to build a project schedule. Some managers want to provide one estimate for each activity while others prefer to provide three estimates for each activity. You decide that the estimate you want to include in the project for each activity is the best estimate of the time required to accomplish the activity accounting for the fact that things don't always occur as normal. This estimate is called:

a. optimistic estimate
b. pessimistic estimate
c. most likely estimate
d. expected time

Solution #17.

Answer (d) is the best answer.

The expected time is the time the activity would take if the activity was repeated over a long period of time.
The optimistic time is the time the activity would take if things proceed better than they normally proceed.
The pessimistic time is the time the activity would take if things proceed worse than they normally proceed.
The most likely time is the time the activity would take if things proceed as normal.

The word "best" makes this tricky. Read the entire phrase: " best estimate of the time required to accomplish the activity accounting for the fact that things don't always occur as normal". Based on the entire phrase we can eliminate answer (c).

Question 18.

As you are developing your project schedule it is suggested that you use PERT to estimate activity durations. You go to the programmer performing Activity A and ask her for her estimates. She states that optimistically Activity A can be completed in 25 days. Most likely Activity A will take 30 days and pessimistically Activity A will take 53 days. What is the PERT estimate you should use when building your schedule?

a. 30 days
b. 33 days
c. 36 days
d. 53 days

Solution #18.

Answer (b) is the best answer.

PERT = (pessimistic + 4*Most likely + optimistic) ÷ 6
PERT = (P+4ML+O) ÷ 6

PERT = (53 + (4*30) +25) ÷ 6
PERT = 33 days

Question #19.

You are managing a project to rebuild a bridge over the Seine River in Paris. There are two activities left on the critical path. Activity A has a pessimistic estimate of 80 days and an optimistic estimate of 62 days. Activity B has a pessimistic estimate of 38 days and an optimistic estimate of 14 days. Assume calculations are based on +/- 3 standard deviations. What is the standard deviation (SD) of the overall remaining path?

a.   5 days
b.   7 days
c. 25 days
d. 30 days

Solution #19. MOST LIKELY THIS QUESTION IS TO DIFFICULT TO BE REPRESENTATIVE OF THE EXAM- though it is possible you could see this.

Answer (a) is the best answer.

Solution: each element of this solution explains one idea in our table.
To solve we usually follow the following steps:
1. Determine duration uncertainty for each activity from pessimistic and optimistic numbers.
   - Duration Uncertainty = P-O
2. Determine the Standard Deviation for each activity.
   One SD = $|(P-O)/6|$.
3. Determine the variance of each activity
   - Variance = $(SD)^2$
4. Calculate the Project Variance (or we could say remaining path)
5. Determine the Standard Deviation for the path
6. Determine duration uncertainty for the remaining path (question did not ask for this)

Activities	P	O	Step 1 Duration Uncertainty	Step 2 One SD	Step3 Variance
Activity A	80	62	18	3	9
Activity B	38	14	24	4	16

Step 4	Variance for Path	Add individual variances together	9+16= 25
Step 5	Standard Deviation for path	Square root of the path variance	Square root of 25 = 5
Step 6	Duration Uncertainty for path	Same as +/-3 SD. Therefore multiple one standard deviation by 6.	5 * 6 = 30 days

Question #20.

Management imposed an end no later than of day 16 on your project. Based on the table below what is the project float?

a. Negative 10 days
b. Negative 9 days
c. Negative 8 days
d. Negative 7 days

Activity	Predecessor	Duration in Days
Activity A	Start	5 days
Activity B	Activity A	3 days
Activity C	Activity A	8 days
Activity D	Activity B and Activity C	1 day
Activity E	Activity D	9 days
Finish	Activity E	Not applicable

Solution #20.

Answer (d) is the best answer.

To solve this question I would draw the network diagram.

Method one.
Paths:
A+B+D+E = 5+3+1+9 =18 days
A+C+D+E = 5+8+1+9 =23 days
Therefore we plan for the project to take 23 days. If management says to finish no later than 16 days we have negative 7 days of project float.

Method Two.
The critical path method.
The diagram shows the earliest I believe the project can finish is day 23.
Now I place the imposed end date (finish no later than) as the late finish of the last activity.
Project float = late finish minus early finish
Project float = 16 - 23 = negative 7 days
Project float = -7 days

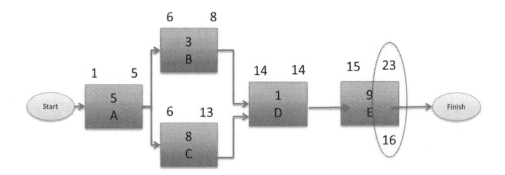

Question #21.

From the figure below what activities are on the critical path?

a. A+B+C+E+G
b. A+B+C+F+G
c. A+B+D+F+G
d. A+B+C+D+E+F+G

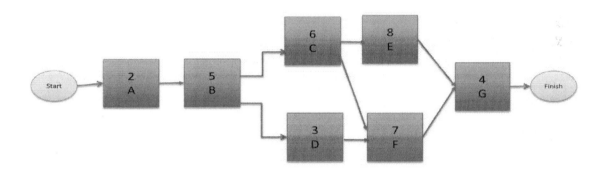

Solution #21.

Answer (a) is the best answer.

There are two methods to determine the anticipated project duration and the activities on the critical path.
Method One:
List all the paths and then determine the longest path (the critical path).
A+B+C+E+G = 2+5+6+8+4 = 25
A+B+C+F+G = 2+5+6+7+4 = 24
A+B+D+F+G = 2+5+3+7+4 = 21.
Be careful of answer (d). This does not represent a real path.
The longest path (in days) is 25 days. Therefore the activities on the critical path are:
A+B+C+E+G

Method Two:
Some people would say the harder way to solve the problem is to use the critical path method. Here is the solution using the critical path. With the critical path method we must complete both the forward and the backward pass. Now we look for activities that have the same early finish and late finish.

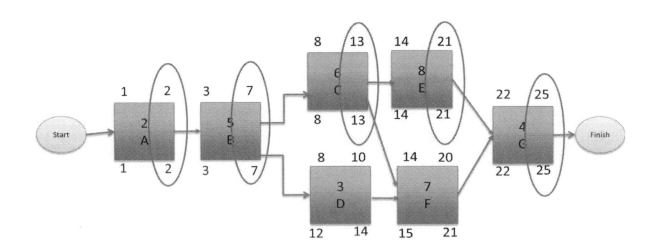

Question #22.

Based on the Activity on Arrow (AoA) Diagram below what is the duration of the critical path?

a. 8 days
b. 19 days
c. 26 days
d. 55 days

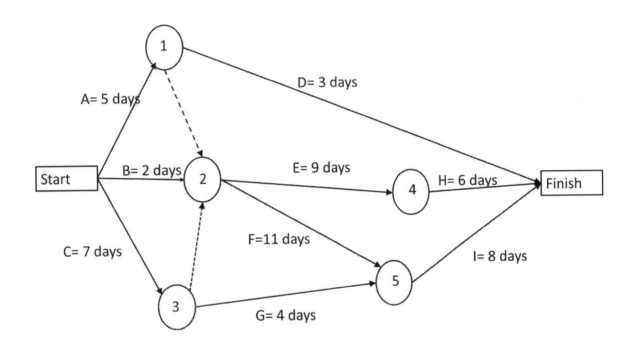

Solution #22.

Answer (c) is the best answer.

This is an Activity on Arrow (AoA) Diagram.
The easiest method to determine the anticipated duration of the project or of the critical path is to determine the paths, the path lengths, and realize the longest path is the critical path and represents the anticipated project duration.

There are multiple paths through the network. Let's calculate the length of each one:
Path A + D = 5+3 = 8 days

Path A + E + H = 5+9+6 = 20 days. Did you even see this path? The dotted arrow is called a dummy activity. It represents a relationship between activities. Dummy activities have no duration and no cost.

Path A + F + I = 5+11+8 = 24 days

Path B + E + H = 2+9+6 = 17 days

Path B + F + I = 2+11+8 = 21 days

Path C + E + H = 7+9+6 = 22 days

Path C + F + I =7+11+8 = 26 days

Path C+ G + I = 7+4+8 = 19 days.

The anticipated project duration is the duration of the longest path.
Therefore the anticipated project duration is 26 days.
Also the anticipated duration of the critical path is 26 days.
The critical path is the longest path through the network and represents the anticipated project duration.

Question #23.

The following information if available for Activity D.
The early start is Day 16.
The duration is 3 days.
The late finish is Day 12.

Therefore we may conclude:

a. Activity D is on the critical path.
b. Activity D has a total slack of negative 6 days.
c. Activity D has a late start of day 7.
d. Activity D is running late.

Solution #23.

Answer (b) is the best answer.

To solve this question I would draw a simple diagram.
This is what the question states.

Early start = day 16	Duration = 3days	
	Activity D	
		Late finish = day 12

This is what I can conclude based on the question.

Early start = day 16	Duration = 3days	Early finish = day 18
	Activity D	
Late start = day 10	Total Float = -6 days	Late finish = day 12

The early start is day 16.   The duration is 3 days.
Therefore the early finish is = 16 +3 -1 = day 18.

The late finish is day 12. The duration is 3 days.
Therefore the late start = 12-3 +1 = day 10.

The late finish is day 12. The early finish is day 18.
Therefore the total float (or we could say total slack) = 12-18 = negative 6 days.

At this point we do not know if Activity D is on the critical path. While it has a negative float there may be other activities that have a larger negative float.

At this point we do not know if Activity D is running late. A negative float on an activity does not mean the activity is running late.

Question #24.

There seems to be confusion in your organization related to the critical path method. The biggest frustration is people not understanding the idea of early and late start and finish dates. One way to explain critical path method is to state:

a. the critical path method is used to determine the exact start and finish dates for every activity

b. the critical path method is used to determine feeder and project buffers to account for limited resources

c. the critical path method is used to ensure that we have a flat use of resources across project activities

d. the critical path method is used to determine the amount of flexibility we have in the schedule

Solution #24.

Answer (d) is the best answer.

The critical path method uses early and late start and finish dates to indicate time periods when activities may occur. These dates do not represent the exact dates of the project.
The critical chain method, not the critical path method, is used to determine buffers to account for limited resources as well as uncertainty. Resource leveling and resource smoothing are used to ensure we have a flat use of resources.

Question #25.

Based on the figure below, what activities are on the critical path?

a. A-B-D-F-H
b. A-B-E-F-H
c. A-B-E-G-H
d. A-C-E-F-H

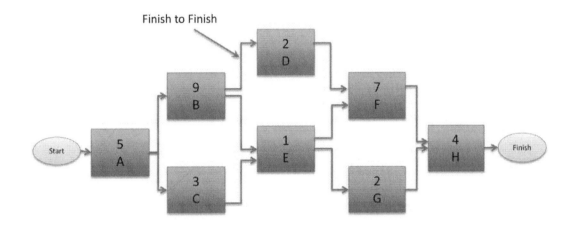

Solution #25.

Answer (b) is the best answer.

There are two methods to determine the anticipated project duration.

Method One: List all the paths and then determine the longest path.
A-B-D-F-H= 5 +9+0+7+4 = 25. Note: (we do not add D's duration since B to D is a finish to finish). We take the large of the two numbers.
A-B-E-F-H = 5+9+1+7+4 = 26
A-B-E-G-H = 5+9+1+2+4 = 21
A-C-E-F-H = 5+3+1+7+4 = 20
A-C-E-G-H =5+3+1+2+4 = 15
The longest path (in days) is 26 days. Therefore the activities on the critical path are: A-B-E-F-H

Method Two. Some people would say the harder way to solve the problem is to use the critical path method. Here is the solution using critical path. With the critical path method we must complete both the forward and the backward pass. Now we look for activities that have the same early finish and late finish.
Note- the late finish of Activity B is 14 because of Activity E not Activity D.

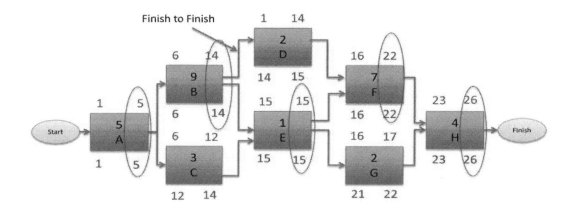

Question #26.

You are developing your project schedule it is suggested that you use formulas based on Beta Distributions to estimate activity durations. You go to the engineer performing Activity A and ask her for her estimates. She states that best-case Activity A can be completed in 25 days. Most likely Activity A will take 32 days and worst-case Activity A will take 49 days. What is the variance for activity A based on the estimates provided?

a. 4 days
b. 16 days
c. 33 days
d. 37 days

Solution #26.

Answer (b) is the best answer.

Variance for an activity = the activity's standard deviation squared.

The standard deviation (SD) for an activity:
SD = | (pessimistic-optimistic) ÷ 6 |.

In this example:
- worst case represents pessimistic
- best case represents optimistic
- we do not need the most likely value.

Therefore:

SD = | (49-25) ÷ 6| = | 24 ÷ 6| = 4

Variance = standard deviation squared

Variance = 4^2 = 16

Question #27.

Your highway construction project is falling behind schedule. Based on our current forecasts it has been decided that we need to pull four weeks out of the schedule. A fund of $6,000 has been provided to cover the cost of crashing. Your critical path includes Activities A, D, F, and K. Activity A is our next activity to perform. Activity K is our last activity. Your team has put together the following table for the activities left to complete on the project.

Activity	Current Duration	Weeks saved by crashing	Cost of crashing	Cost/week of crashing
Activity A	6 weeks	2 weeks	$4,000	$2,000
Activity D	3 weeks	1 week	$1,000	$1,000
Activity F	4 weeks	1 week	$1,000	$1,000
Activity K	8 weeks	2 weeks	$4,000	$2,000
Activity M	6 weeks	2 weeks	$2,000	$1,000
Activity P	8 weeks	2 weeks	$2,000	$1,000

What activities are you most likely to crash?

a. Activities A and M
b. Activities D, F, M and P
c. Activities D, F and K
d. Activities A, D, F

Solution #27.

Answer (d) is the best answer.

A few rules about crashing:

1. Only crash activities on the critical path
2. Crash the activities on the critical path that save the most amount of time for the least amount of money
3. Crash an early activity instead of a later activity if they have the same amount of time saved for the same money

Based on Item 1 above we should not crash Activity M and P since they are not on the critical path. We have now eliminated Answer (a) and answer (b).

If we look at answer (c) we can save 4 weeks for $6,000.
If we look at answer (d) we can save 4 weeks for $6,000.

Using rule 3 above we will want to crash Activity A before Activity K since Activity A comes before Activity K on the critical path.

Question #28.

As you are developing your project schedule it is suggested that you use PERT to estimate activity durations. You go to the programmer performing Activity A and ask her for her estimates. She states that best-case Activity A can be completed in 25 days. Most likely Activity A will take 30 days and worst-case Activity A will take 55 days. What is the standard deviation for Activity A?

a.   5 days
b. 25 days
c. 33 days
d. 36 days

Solution #28.

Answer (a) is the best answer.

Standard Deviation (SD) for an activity:

SD = |(P-O) ÷ 6|
P = pessimistic (worst case in this example)
O = optimistic (best case in this example)

SD = | (55 – 25) ÷ 6 |
SD = | (30) ÷ 6 |
The standard deviation = 5 days

Question #29.

 You are managing a project to rebuild a bridge over the Rio Grande. There are two activities left on the critical path. Activity Y has a duration uncertainty of 36 days. Activity Z has a duration uncertainty of 54 days. Assume calculations are based on +/- 3 standard deviations. What is the duration uncertainty for the remainder of the critical path?

a.   10 days
b.   15 days
c.   65 days
d.   90 days

Solution #29.

Answer (c) is the best answer.

Solution: each element of this solution explains one idea in our table.
To solve we usually use the following steps:
1. determine duration uncertainty for each activity from pessimistic and optimistic numbers. We don't need to do this as it was a given.
   - Duration uncertainty = P-O
2. determine the Standard Deviation for each activity.
   One SD = |(P-O)/6|.
3. Determine the variance of each activity
   - Variance = (SD)^2
4. Calculate the Project Variance
5. Determine the Standard Deviation for the path
6. Determine duration uncertainty for the remaining path

Activities	P	O	Step 1 Duration Uncertainty	Step 2 One SD	Step3 Variance
Activity Y			36	6	36
Activity Z			54	9	81

Step 4	Variance for Path (project variance going forward)	Add individual variances together	=36 + 81 = 117
Step 5	Standard Deviation for path	Square root of the path variance	Square root of 117 = 10.8
Step 6	Duration Uncertainty for path	Same as +/-3 SD. Therefore multiple one standard deviation by 6.	10.8 * 6 = 64.8 days

Question #30.

As the project manager you are working with team members to estimate activity durations. The engineer who will be responsible for Activity A states that most likely it will take 31 days to complete Activity A. Best case it may be completed in 25 days and worst case it could take as long as 43 days.
Your schedule management plan states that you will use the triangular distribution for your three point estimate. Based on this your estimate for Activity A is:

a. 31 days
b. 32 days
c. 33 days
d. 43 days

Solution #30.

Answer (c) is the best answer.

The triangular distribution is another name for a simple average.
Simple Average Estimate = (Pessimistic +Most Likely + Optimistic) ÷3.
In this question we can assume:
worst case = pessimistic
best case = optimistic

Simple Average Estimate = (43 + 31 + 25) ÷ 3.
Simple Average Estimate = 99÷3.
Simple Average Estimate = 33 days.

Question #31.

Management has stated that the project must be complete in 22 days total. Based on the diagram below what is the project float?

a. + 3 days
b. + 2 days
c. - 2 days
d. - 3 days

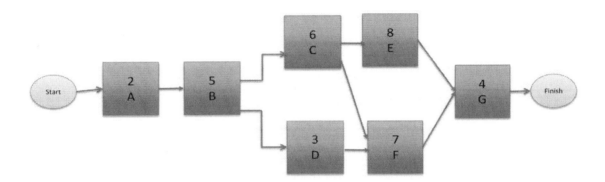

Solution #31.

Answer (d) is the best answer.

There are two methods to determine the anticipated project duration.

Method One:
List all the paths and then determine the longest path (the critical path).
There are two ways to solve the problem.
Paths:
A+B+C+E+G = 2+5+6+8+4 = 25
A+B+C+F+G = 2+5+6+7+4 = 24
A+B+D+F+G = 2+5+3+7+4 = 21.

The longest path (in days) is 25 days. Management states that we must finish in 22 days. Therefore the project float is 22 days minus 25 days = negative 3 days. Does the negative sign make sense? We expect to finish in 25 days. Management says finish in 22 days. If we stay on our plan we will be 3 days late.

Method Two:
Some people would say the harder way to solve the problem is to use the critical path method. Here is the solution using the critical path method. With the critical path method we must complete only the forward pass. Then we place the 22 days from management as the late finish of the last activity.

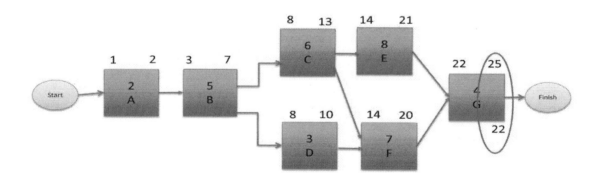

Question #32.

At this point your project is falling weeks behind schedule. There are no additional resources available. Based on the anticipated market for the products it is worth taking more risk in order to achieve the original schedule. Most likely you will:

a. resource level
b. resource smooth
c. crash
d. fast track

Solution #32.

Answer (d) is the best answer.

Fast Tracking a schedule allows for the overlap of activities on the critical path. One of the positives of fast tracking is that it provides the opportunity to shorten the schedule. One of the major negatives of fast tracking is that it increases the overall project risk. We would only fast track when the reward is worth the risk.

Resource leveling is used to balance the demand for resources with the supply available. Resource leveling does not shorten the schedule and in many cases resource leveling makes the planned schedule longer.

Resource smoothing is also used to balance the demand for resources with the supply available. Resource smoothing does not shorten the schedule. It does not lengthen the schedule either as one of the tenants of resource smoothing is that the project end date is not allowed to shift. Resource smoothing does not always balance the demand with the supply.

Based on the information provided we cannot crash the schedule. Crashing the schedule requires additional resources that are not available.

Question 33.

From the figure below what is the Total Float of Activity C? Assume all durations are in days.

a. 2 days
b. 5 days
c. 6 days
d. 0 days

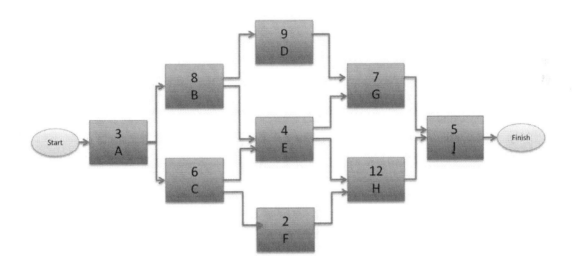

Solution #33.

Answer (a) is the best answer.

We use the critical path method to solve for total float. We need to perform both a forward pass and a backward pass.

Total Float of Activity C = Late Finish of C – Early Finish of C
Total Float of Activity C = 11-9
Total Float of Activity C = 2 days

On the exam, especially if I was pressed for time I may not bother with the critical path method on this diagram. It is clear from the Diagram:
- Activity A must be on the critical path.
- Either Activity B or Activity C must be on the critical path. Since Activity B is 2 days longer than Activity C we know that Activity B must be on the critical path and Activity C has 2 days of total float. This diagram is clear and easy. If the diagram was not so clear I would use the critical path.

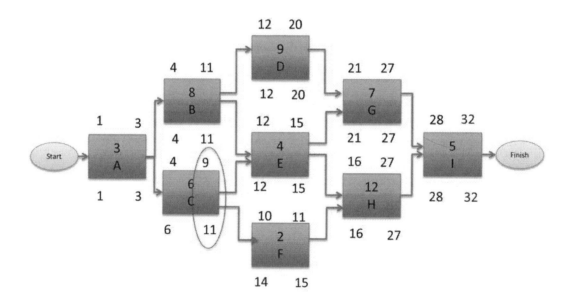

Question # 34.

From the figure below what is the total slack of Activity E?

a. 0 days
b. 4 days
c. 6 days
d. 9 days

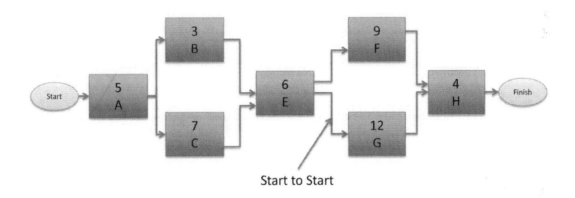

Start to Start

Solution #34.

Answer (a) is the best answer.

Method one.
We don't need to do a forward and backward pass to solve. The question asks for total slack. Remember:
Total Slack = Total Float = Slack = Float.

The total float of Activity E must be zero since Activity E is on the critical path. Activity E must be on the critical path since there is no other way through the network but to go through Activity E.

Method two.
Some people would complete the forward pass and the backward pass to solve the question. I would not perform a forward and backward pass on the exam for this question and therefore I did not perform them here.

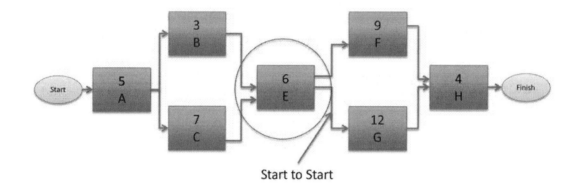

Start to Start

Question $35.

Based on the diagram below what activities are on the critical path?

a. B+D+F+H
b. B +E+F+H
c. B+ E+G+H
d. B+D+E+F+G+H

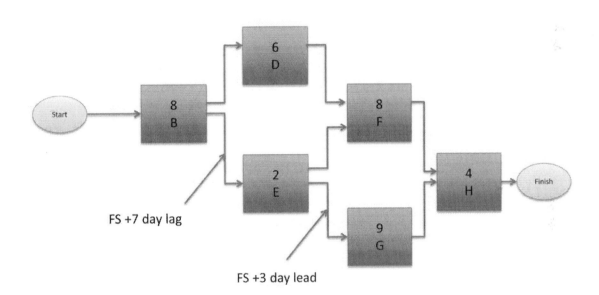

Solution #35.

Answer (b) is the best answer.

There are two methods to determine the anticipated project duration.
Method One:
List all the paths and then determine the longest path (the critical path).
Paths:
B+D+F+H = 8+6+8+4 = 26 days
B+7day lag +E + F + H = 8+7+2+8+4 = 29 days
B+7day lag + E +(-3 days) +G + H = 8+7+2-3+9+4 = 27
The path of 29 days is the longest path.
Therefore the activities on the critical path are: B + E + F +H.

Method Two:
Use the critical path method. Perform both a forward and a backward
pass. Since we are in planning look for early starts = late starts. You may
look for early finishes = late finishes. During planning the critical path is
the path with zero float. If the late start of an activity equals the early
start the activity has zero float. If the late finish equals the early finish the
activity has zero float.

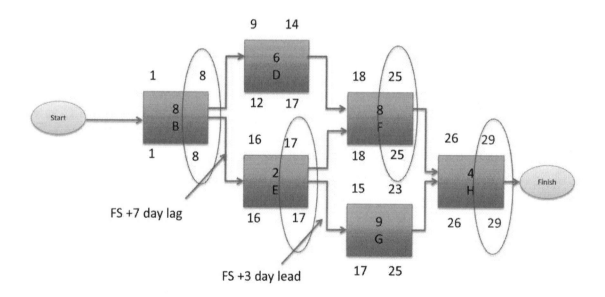

Question #36.

Based on the activity on arrow (AoA) diagram below what is the duration of the critical path? Assume all durations are in days.

a. 12 days
b. 33 days
c. 35 days
d. 38 days

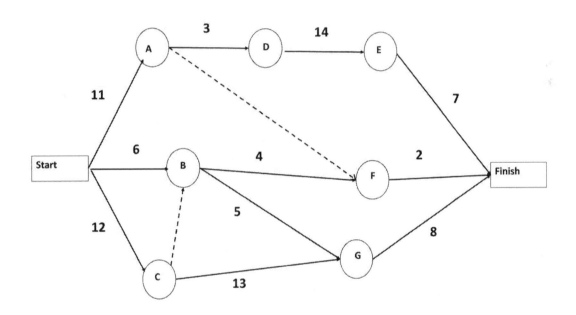

Solution #36.

Answer (c) is the best answer.

To determine the anticipated length of the project or the critical path we must determine all the paths, determine the lengths of all the paths and then determine the longest (the critical) path.

We have set up the solution as a table to make our ideas a little clearer (we hope).

Path	Durations	Path Duration
Start-A-D-E-Finish	11+3+14+7	35 days
Start-A-F-Finish	11+0+2	13 days
Start-B-F-Finish	6+4+2	12 days
Start-B-G-Finish	6+5+8	19 days
Start-C-B-F-Finish	12+0+4+2	18 days
Start-C-B-G-Finish	12+0+5+8	25 days
Start-C-G-Finish	12+13+8	33 days

Therefore the longest path in days is 35 days. The anticipated length of the project or the critical path is 35 days.

Question #37.

You are developing your project schedule it is suggested that you use formulas based on Beta Distributions (PERT) to estimate activity durations. You go to the programmer performing Activity A and ask her for her estimates. She states that optimistically Activity A can be completed in 13 days. Most likely Activity A will take 17 days and pessimistically Activity A will take 43 days. What is the variance for activity A based on the estimates provided?

a.   5 days
b. 19 days
c. 21 days
d. 25 days

Solution #37.

Answer (d) is the best answer..

Variance for an activity = the activity's standard deviation squared.

The standard deviation (SD) for an activity:
SD = | (pessimistic-optimistic) ÷ 6 |.

In this example we do not need the most likely value.

Therefore:

SD = | (43-13) ÷ 6| = | 30 ÷ 6| = 5

Variance = standard deviation squared

Variance = 5^2 = 25

Question #38.

Our project schedule shows work continuing for over four years. We have determined our critical path. We also have defined the parameters used to determine near-critical paths. Which of the following is true related to critical and near-critical paths?

a. a critical path may not have any lags
b. a critical path may not have any leads
c. a project may only have one critical path
d a project may have multiple near critical paths

Solution #38.

Answer (d) is the best answer.

The project manager along with the project management staff should determine the criteria for a path to be declared a near critical path. Having multiple near critical paths provides added risk on the project. Critical paths, and near critical paths may include both leads and lags. Do not confuse the word "float" with the words "leads and lags". Float means flexibility.
The critical path is the longest path through the network. If you have more than one path with the same length that represent the longest path(s) through the network they would all be called critical paths.
Based on your criteria you may have more than one near critical path.

Question #39.

You are managing a project to rebuild a bridge over the River Nile in Egypt. There are four activities left on the critical path. Activity W has a pessimistic estimate of 80 days and an optimistic estimate of 50 days. Activity X has a pessimistic estimate of 68 days and an optimistic estimate of 44 days. Activity Y has a pessimistic estimate of 26 days and an optimistic estimate of 14 days. Activity Z has a pessimistic estimate of 46 days and an optimistic estimate of 34 days. Assume calculations are based on +/- 3 standard deviations. What is the standard deviation (SD) of the overall remaining path?

a. 7 days
b. 42 days
c. 49 days
d. 78 days

Solution #39. THE QUESTION IS MOST LIKELY TO DIFFICULT TO BE REPRESENTATIVE OF THE EXAM. This kind of question is possible though.

Answer (a) is the best answer.

Solution: each element of this solution explains one idea in our table.
To solve we usually use the following steps:
1. Determine duration uncertainty for each activity from pessimistic and optimistic numbers. We don't need to do this as it was a given.
   - Duration uncertainty = P-O
2. Determine the Standard Deviation for each activity.
   One SD = |(P-O)/6|.
3. Determine the variance of each activity
   - Variance = (SD)²
4. Calculate the Project Variance (or we could say variance for the remaining path)
5. Determine the Standard Deviation for the path
6. Determine duration uncertainty for the remaining path (this question did not ask for duration uncertainty)

Activities	P	O	Step 1 Duration Uncertainty	Step 2 One SD	Step3 Variance
Activity W	80	50	30	5	25
Activity X	68	44	24	4	16
Activity Y	26	14	12	2	4
Activity Z	46	34	12	2	4

Step 4	Variance for Path	Add individual variances together	25+16+4+4= 49
Step 5	Standard Deviation for path	Square root of the path variance	Square root of 49 = 7
Step 6- not required to solve this question	Duration Uncertainty for path	Same as +/-3 SD. Therefore multiple one standard deviation by 6.	7 * 6 = 42 days

Question #40.

Based on your project management experience you realize that the term float and the term slack both mean the "extra" time available to complete an activity. Now your risk manager is asking you about "free float". Free float is:

a. the amount of time an activity may be delayed without delaying the entire project

b. the amount of time an activity may be delayed without delaying the critical path

c. the amount of time an activity may be delayed without delaying any immediate successors

d. the amount of time an activity may be delayed without having to spend extra money

Solution #40.

Answer (c) is the best answer.

Free float is a subset of total float (or we could say total slack). Total float is how much time an activity may be delayed before it would delay the entire project (or we could say delay the critical path). Delaying the critical path is delaying the entire project completion.
Free float is the amount of total float that is free. When we say free we mean the amount of time an activity may be delayed without delaying any other activity. The word "free" in this context is not related to money.

Question #41.

The free float of Activity C in the diagram below is:

a. 0 days
b. 3 days
c. 6 days
d. 7 days

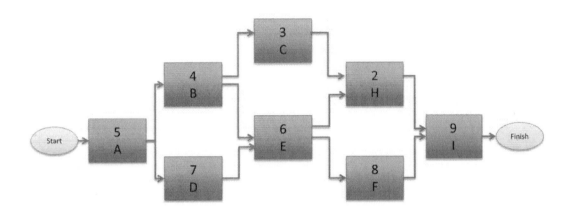

Solution #41.

Answer (c) is the best answer.

Some of us would like to solve this by just looking at the diagram. For many of us this will bring us to the wrong answer.
From my view to solve for free float of an activity we need to perform a forward path.

Free float = Early Start of successor minus Early Finish of current activity minus one.
In this example:
Free Float = Early Start of Activity H minus Early Finish of Activity C minus 1.
Free Float = 19-12-1
Free Float = 6 days.

Note that this question did not tell us that the durations were in days. Based on the answers there is no other conclusion to draw. The durations must be in days.

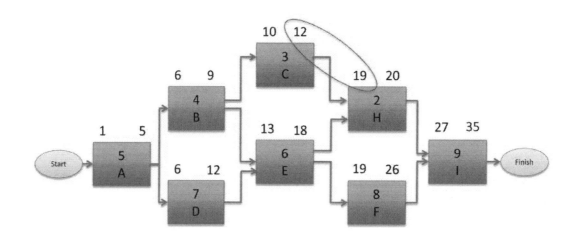

Question #42.

What activities are on the critical path in the diagram below? Assume all durations are in days.

a. A+B+D+F
b. A+B+E+F
c. A+C+E+F
d. A+C+G

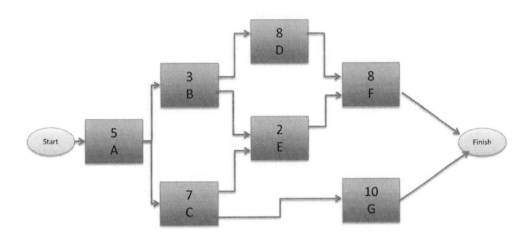

Solution #42.

Answer (a) is the best answer.

The critical path is the longest path through the network. There are two methods to solve this problem.
Method One. Determine the length of each path. The activities on the longest path are the activities on the critical path.
A+B+D+F = 5+3+8+8 =24
A+B+E+F = 5+3+2+8 = 18
A+C+E+F = 5+7+2+8 = 22
A+C+G = 5+7+10 =22
Therefore the critical path is A+B+D+F = 24 days.

Method Two. The critical Path Method.
The other method to solve is to perform a forward pass and a backward pass using the critical path method. During planning the activities that have the same early start and late start, or the same early finish and late finish are on the critical path.

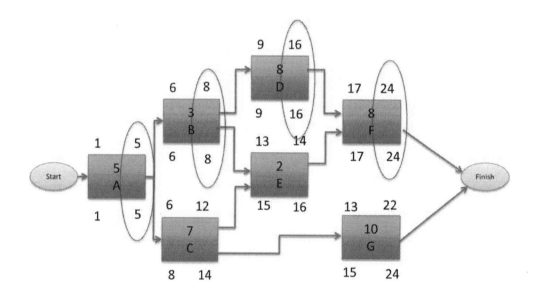

Question #43.

Based on the diagram below; If management imposes a constraint to end no later than day 25 what is the new total slack on Activity F? Assume all durations are in days.

a. -4 days
b. -3 days
c. +3 days
d. +4 days

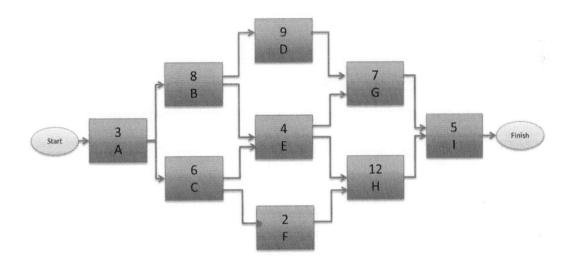

Solution #43.

Answer (b) is the best answer.

To solve this problem we need to do a forward pass. Hopefully you realize you have already completed a forward and a backward pass on this diagram. See Question and Solution 33. On the Exam some network diagrams may be repeated as the basis for different questions.

If I could not find my old diagram or decided to start anew I would do the forward pass and then only the backward pass based on the imposed end date.

If I could find my old diagram (see below) I would now change the late finish of Activity I to Day 25 (management's end no later than date).
Now we must perform a new backward pass beginning with the late finish of Activity I being Day 25. Please see below, Notice that I just perform the backward pass to get me to Activity F. I don't bother to update my numbers for Activities A, B, C, D, E, and G as that work is not required to solve the problem.
Project Float of Activity F = Late finish of Activity F minus Early Finish of Activity F.
Project Float of Activity F = 8 – 11 = -3 days

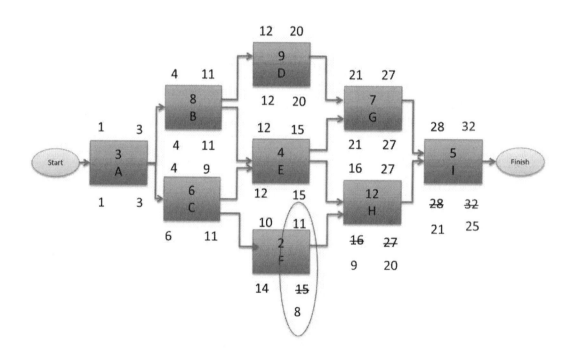

Question #44.

The planning for your project is going very well. Management believes you will have plenty of project float. They have imposed that you finish no later than Day 29. Based on the table below what is your project float?

a. + 6 days
b. – 6 days
c. + 5 days
d. – 5 days

Activity	Successor	Duration in Days
Start	A	Not applicable
Activity A	Activity B and Activity C	5 days
Activity B	Activity D	3 days
Activity C	Activity D	8 days
Activity D	Activity E	1 days
Activity E	Finish	9 days

Solution #44.

Answer (a) is the best answer.

To solve this question I would draw a network diagram. Notice the table provides the successor for activities, not the predecessors.
Method one.
List the paths to determine the planned length of the project.
A+B+D+E = 5+3+1+9 = 18
A+C+D+E = 5+8+1+9 = 23
The longest path is 23 days. If management imposes an end no later than day 29 we have 6 days of positive float.

Method two.
Perform a forward pass using the critical path method. The network diagram shows that we believe the project can finish no earlier than Day 23. Management says to finish no later than Day 29.
Project float= late finish minus early finish
Project float= 29 − 23 = 6 days.
If we stay on the early dates of our schedule the project will finish 6 days early.

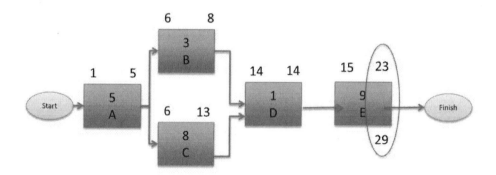

Question #45.

Your organization has been using activity on node (AoN) precedence diagrams for years. A new project manager has joined the group and is pushing for activity on arrow (AoA) diagrams. You remember that activity on arrow (AoA) diagrams utilize dummy activities to represent dependencies between tasks. Most organizations have not adopted activity on arrow (AoA) diagrams because these diagrams only allow for:

a. finish to start relationships
b. finish to finish relationships
c. start to start relationships
d. start to finish relationships

Solution #45.

Answer (a) is the best answer.

Activity on arrow (AoA) diagrams only allow for finish to start relationships. This is one of the big drawbacks of AoA diagrams and the primary reason most organizations do not use these diagrams.

Conversely Activity on Node (AoN) diagrams allow for all four types of relationships and therefore AoN is a much more common way of representing a network diagram. The four types of relationships allowed with an Activity on Node (AoN) diagram are:

- Finish to start
- Finish to finish
- Start to start
- Start to finish

Question #46.

As the project manager you are working with team members to estimate activity durations. The engineer who will be responsible for Activity A states that most likely it will take 31 days to complete Activity A. Best case it may be completed in 25 days and worst case it could take as long as 43 days.
Your schedule management plan states that you will use the beta distribution for your three point estimate. Based on this your three point estimate for Activity A is:

a. 31 days
b. 32 days
c. 33 days
d. 43 days

Solution #46.

Answer (b) is the best answer.

The beta distribution is from the traditional PERT technique.

PERT Estimate = (Pessimistic +4*Most Likely + Optimistic) ÷6.
In this question we can assume:
worst case = pessimistic
best case = optimistic

PERT Estimate = (43 + (4*31) + 25) ÷6.
PERT Estimate = 192÷6.
PERT Estimate = 32 days

Question #47.

Based on the following table what is the anticipated critical path for the network?

a. Start-A-B-G-Finish
b. Start-E-F-Finish
c. Start-A-D-G-Finish
d. Start-A-B-C-Finish

Activity	Duration in Days
Start-A	2
A-B	5
B-C	9
B-G	0
C-Finish	10
Start-D	4
A-D	0
D-G	6
G-Finish	11
Start-E	3
E-G	0
E-F	8
F-Finish	12

Solution #47.

Answer (d) is the best answer.

Based on the table we can assume this is an Activity on Arrow (AoA) Diagram. To determine the critical path we need to:
1. Draw the AoA diagram
2. Determine the paths
3. Determine the length of the paths
4. The longest path is the critical path

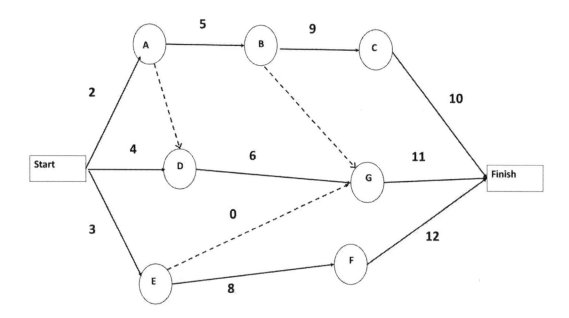

Paths	Durations	Path Duration
Start-A-B-C-Finish	2+5+9+10	26
Start-A-D-G-Finish	2+0+6+11	19
Start-A-B-G-Finish	2+5+0+11	18
Start-D-G-Finish	4+6+11	21
Start-E-G-Finish	3+0+11	14
Start-E-F-Finish	3+8+12	23

Therefore the longest path is: Start-A-B-C-Finish. This is the critical path. The planned length of the critical path is 26 days.

Question #48.

Based on the figure below what activities are on the critical path?

a. A+B+D+F
b. A+B+E+F
c. A+C+E+F
d. A+B+C+D+E+F

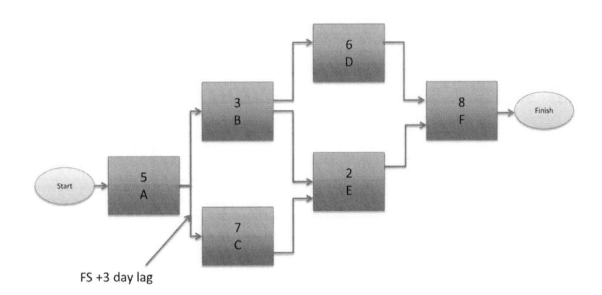

FS +3 day lag

Solution #48.

Answer (c) is the best answer.

There are two methods to determine what activities are on the critical path.
Method One:
List all the paths and then determine the longest path (the critical path).
A+B+D+F = 5+3+6+8 = 22 days
A+B+E+F = 5+3+2+8 = 18 days
A+ lag of 3 days + C+ E + F = 5+3day lag + 7+2+8 = 25 days.
The path of 25 days is the longest path.
Therefore the activities on the critical path are : A + C + E + F

Method Two:
Use the critical path method. Perform both a forward and a backward pass. Since we are in planning look for early starts = late starts or early finishes = late finishes.

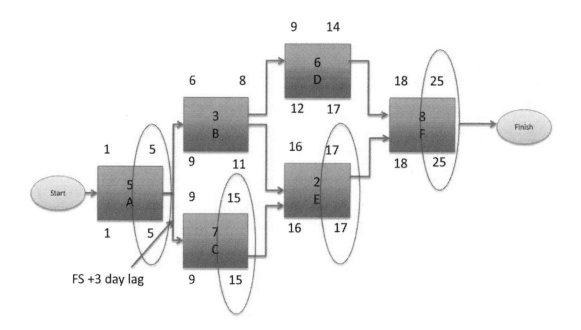

Question# 49.

From the diagram below determine the Free Float of Activity F. Assume all durations are in days.

a. 25 days
b. 14 days
c.   3 days
d.   0 days

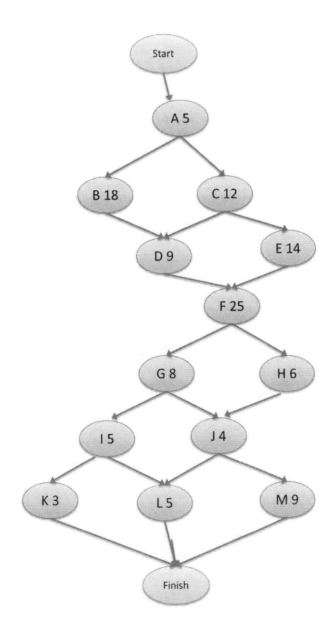

Solution #49.

Answer (d) is the best answer.

Wow. What a diagram. Realize that network diagrams may be drawn many different ways. The convention is to use boxes for precedence diagrams. There is no reason though that someone could not draw the diagram with circles or ovals or any shape.
Did you go ahead and complete a forward pass to solve this problem? If you did that was a lot of work, a lot of wasted work. Let's look at Activity F. Can you determine just from looking at the diagram that Activity F must be on the critical path? During planning the total float of any activity on the critical path is zero as long as there is no imposed end date. If the total float of Activity F is zero what is the free float? Free float can never be greater than total float. Therefore if the total float of Activity F is zero the free float must also be zero.

Free float is a subset of total float. Therefore the free float of an activity can never be greater than its total float.

Question #50.

Your manager comes to you and states that you need to finish the project at least four weeks early. At this point you should:

a. crash as soon as possible
b. fast track all activities on and off the critical path
c. evaluate the change request and create options
d. determine the best areas to de-scope the project

Solution #50.

Answer (c) is the best answer.

This can be a tricky question for some. Hopefully through your studies you realize that we should treat situations like this as change requests. We should evaluate the change request and come back with options including our recommendation. Most likely we will need more information to evaluate the change request.

Answer (a) states to crash as soon as possible. Be careful of answers with the phrase "as soon as possible". We hardly would do anything "as soon as possible". In most situations we would begin with an evaluation and option creation.

Answer (b) says to fast track all activities on and off the critical path. Be careful of the word "all". Also if we are trying to shorten the schedule fast tracking activities that are not on the critical path will only increase our risk without actually shortening the schedule.

Answer (d) states that we should determine the best areas to de-scope. At this point we don't know if we need to de-scope. There are multiple ways to address trying to pull in the schedule. De-scoping is one way. Crashing is another way. Fast-tracking is a third way. We need to evaluate the change request before we can jump right to de-scoping.

Bonus question #1.

This bonus question comes from:
How to get every Earned Value Management Question right on the PMP®
Exam – PMP Exam Prep Simplified Series of mini-e-books
(50+ PMP® Exam Prep Sample Questions and Solutions
on Earned Value Management)
(AME Group 2014)

You are taking over the role of project manager on a project to build a training facility for horses. Earned value management (EVM) is being used on the project and you have been handed some incomplete information. For your project, the cost performance index (CPI) = 1.2. The actual cost (AC) = $75,000. The planned value (PV) = $60,000. What is the earned value (EV) for this project?

a. $50,000
b. $62,500
c. $72,000
d. $90,000

Bonus Solution #1.

Answer (d) is the best answer.

This is an equation manipulation question. If you look at your equation list you probably do not have an equation to calculate earned value (EV). In this question we are given the cost performance index (CPI), the actual cost (AC), and the planned value (PV). We are asked to calculate earned value (EV). Do you have an equation with three of these terms including earned value (EV)? Most likely you have the equation:

$CPI = EV/AC$.
We want to solve for EV. Therefore, we want to get EV alone on one side of the equal sign. Multiply both sides of the equation by AC.
$AC * CPI = AC * (EV/AC)$. The two ACs will eliminate each other on the right side of the equation.
$AC * CPI = EV$.
$\$75,000 (1.2) = EV$
$\$90,000 = EV$

Note that we did not use PV to answer this question. On the exam, we may be given data that we do not need to solve the problem. I call this distractor information.

From a common sense standpoint I see that my CPI > 1. This means the project is running under budget. Therefore the earned value (EV) must be greater than the actual cost (AC). Answer (d) is the only answer with an earned value (EV) greater than the Actual cost (AC) of $75,000.

Bonus Question #2.

A Fixed Price Incentive Fee (FPIF) contract has the following parameters:
Target Cost = $200,000
Target Profit = $20,000
Target Price = $220,000
Ceiling Price = $250,000
Share Ratio 70/30

The project was completed for an actual cost of $170,000. What is the actual profit the seller receives?

a. $9,000
b. $11,000
c. $20,000
d. $29,000

Bonus Solution #2.

Answer (d) is the best answer.

I solve FPIF problems that ask about actual profit and/or actual price by asking and answering a set of questions:
Q. What is the contract type?
A. FPIF

Q. Do we have an over run or under run and by how much?
A. The target cost is $200,000. Make sure you always look at target cost and not target price.
The actual cost is $170,000.
There is an under run of $30,000.

Q. Will the profit be adjusted up or down and by how much?
A. Since there is an under run the seller's profit will be adjusted up by the seller's percentage of the under run. The seller's percentage is 30%. The seller's percentage is always the second number of the share ratio. The adjustment to the seller's profit will be 30% of $30,000.
Profit adjustment = 30% * $30,000 = $9,000.

Q. What is the actual profit?
A. Actual profit = target profit + profit adjustment. The $9,000 is being added since there is an under run. The seller is being rewarded for the under run.
Actual profit = $20,000 + $9,000
Actual profit = $29,000
Since there is an under run we do not need to check the actual price against the ceiling price.

Bonus Question #3.

This bonus question comes from:

How to get every Financial Question right on the PMP® Exam – PMP Exam
Prep Simplified Series of mini-e-books
(50+ PMP® Exam Prep Sample Questions and Solutions
on NPV, IRR, ROI, Etc.)
(AME Group Coming late 2015)

The portfolio review board is conducting a project selection review. They are going to make their decision based on the Net Present Value (NPV) estimates for the projects. The organization has only $100,000 available for investment. Based on the following information which project should they select?
Assume an interest rate of 5%.
Project A –
- The initial investment = $100,000.
- The benefit at the end of year one = $40,000.
- The additional benefit at end of year two = $70,000.
- There are no other benefits.
Project B –
- The initial investment = $100,000.
- There is no benefit at the end of year one.
- The benefit = $42,000 at end of year two.
- There is an additional benefit = $70,000 at end of year 3.

Which project(s) should they select?

a. Project A with a positive net present value
b. Project B with a positive net present value
c. Project A with a negative net present value
d. Project b with a negative net present value

Bonus Solution #3.

Answer (a) is the best answer.

Project A has a higher Net Present Value (NPV) than Project B. The NPV of Project A is a positive number. This means our estimates show we forecast to make a profit on this project.

Project A

The Present Value of $40,000 received at the end of year 1:

$PV = FV/(1+i)^t$

$PV = \$40,000/(1.05)^1$

$PV = \$38,095$

The Present Value of $70,000 received at the end of year 2:

$PV = FV/(1+i)^t$

$PV = \$70,000/(1.05)^2$

$PV = \$63,492$

Therefore the NPV for Project A= $38,095+$63,492 -$100,000= positive $1,587

Project B

Project B is expected to lose money.

The Present Value of $42,000 received at the end of year 2:

$PV = FV/(1+i)^t$

$PV = \$42,000/(1.05)^2$

$PV = \$38,095$

The Present Value of $70,000 received at the end of year 3:

$PV = FV/(1+i)^t$

$PV = \$70,000/(1.05)^3$

$PV = \$60,468$

Therefore the NPV for Project B= $38,095+$60,468-$100,000= negative $1,437

Thank you for reading!

Dear Reader,

I hope you enjoyed my mini book: *How to get every Network Diagram Question right on the exam.* I really enjoy helping people prepare for the PMP® Exam and I hope I helped you. Most importantly I hope the book is useful to you both for the PMP® Exam and for your project management career.

I wanted to request a small favor. If you were so inclined I'd love a review of *How to get every Network Diagram Question right on the PMP exam* on Amazon. Loved it, hated it (I hope not) - I would just enjoy to hear your feedback.

As you may have seen with Amazon, reviews can be tough to come by these days. You the reader have the power now to make or break a book. If you have time I would love you to go back to Amazon and write a quick review of the book. Thank you so much for reading for my mini book: *How to get every Network Diagram right on the PMP® exam.*

To write a review just go back to amazon and my book and click on reviews. Let me know if you would like to see more of these mini books. Specifically tell me the topics you would like covered and the language (English, Spanish, Portuguese, etc.) you will be using for your test.

Realize that along with the mini books I have a full study guide. Currently I am developing an online PMP® Workshop that matches PMP® Exam Prep Live with Aileen Workshop.
Stay in touch and let me know how to best help you. Visit my website www.aileenellis.com for free blogs and videos on preparing for the PMP® Exam.
Regards,

Aileen
aileen@aileenellis.com

Made in the USA
Lexington, KY
18 October 2017